on track ...
Anthony Phillips
1977-1990

every album, every song

Alan Draper

sonicbondpublishing.com

Sonicbond Publishing Limited
www.sonicbondpublishing.co.uk
Email: info@sonicbondpublishing.co.uk

First Published in the United Kingdom 2025
First Published in the United States 2025

British Library Cataloguing in Publication Data:
A Catalogue record for this book is available from the British Library

Copyright Alan Draper 2025

ISBN 978-1-78952-356-0

The right of Alan Draper to be identified
as the author of this work has been asserted by him
in accordance with the Copyright, Designs and Patents Act 1988.
All rights reserved. No part of this publication may be reproduced, stored in a
retrieval system or transmitted in any form or by any means, electronic, mechanical,
photocopying, recording or otherwise, without prior permission in writing from
Sonicbond Publishing Limited

Typeset in ITC Garamond Std & ITC Avant Garde Gothic
Printed and bound in England

Graphic design and typesetting: Full Moon Media

on track ...
Anthony Phillips
1977-1990

every album, every song

Alan Draper

sonicbondpublishing.com

Acknowledgements

First off, my heartfelt thanks go out to Stephen Lambe for bestowing upon me this dream assignment for a lifelong Genesis fan – that of exploring the early output of one of that band's most precociously talented original members: Anthony Phillips. I'd also like to say *Arigato* to Saeki iitsuka in Japan for aiding me in this project via the excellent service provided by Japazon. Many thanks, as always, to my old friend and bandmate Tim Scott for support and encouragement. Special love and thanks to my beautiful wife, Radiance, and to my wider family for their constant support during the writing of this book.

During my research, the following sources have proved invaluable: the fine website *anthonyphillips.co.uk* is packed with interesting information on Ant's career and musical output; Alan Hewitt's website *twronline.net* has, for many years, been a mine of information on Ant and all things Genesis; the website *loudersound.com* also contained some useful articles on Ant and, of course, the wonderful Anthony Phillips CD box sets issued by Esoteric Records were central to this project, as they include additional music, much of it previously unreleased, recorded during the pre-1991 period of Ant's canon, which is covered in this book. These box sets all include copiously detailed sleeve notes and recording data lovingly collated by Jonathan Dann.

The following books were also useful reference points for Ant's early life and his period with Genesis: *I Know What I Like* – Armando Gallo (D.I.Y. Books, 1980); *Genesis: On Track* – Stuart Macfarlane (Sonicbond Publishing, 2022); *The Living Years* – Mike Rutherford (Constable, 2014); *My Book Of Genesis* – Richard Macphail (Wymar Publishing, 2018); *The Songs Of Genesis* – Steve Aldous (McFarland & Co, 2020) and, of course, the indispensable Genesis tome, *Chapter And Verse* – the story of Genesis, as told in the band's words and edited by Philip Dodd (Weidenfeld & Nicolson, Orion Books, 2007) – all these books are heartily recommended to readers with an interest in all things Genesis-related.

In this book, I've covered Ant's original album releases over the period 1977 to 1990 but have also included other recordings taped in this era – that were made available after this period – via the bonus discs *Private Parts & Extra Pieces* and *Private Parts & Extra Pieces II*, included with the Esoteric Records rereleases of Ant's earlier *Private Parts & Pieces* albums. Also covered is the excellent Esoteric Records 2022 release *Archive Collection Volume I & Volume II*, featuring many outtakes from Ant's 1977 to 1990 canon of music.

As I was working on the final chapters of this book, the sad news broke of the passing of Richard Macphail. He was, of course, lead vocalist with Ant's pre-Genesis Charterhouse band, The Anon, as well as Genesis' chief cook and bottle washer during their vital formative period at Christmas Cottage and their faithful road manager between 1969 and 1973. Without Richard, it's doubtful whether Genesis would've gone on to their celebrated later achievements, especially in the wake of Ant's departure from the group in July 1970, when it was only Richard's constant encouragement and optimism that persuaded them to carry on. All Genesis fans owe him a huge debt of gratitude and I personally remember him well from those early Genesis gigs that I was lucky enough to attend. I would, therefore, like to dedicate this book to the memory of Richard Macphail (1950 – 2024).

on track ...
Anthony Phillips
1977-1990

Contents

Introduction 9
The Geese & The Ghost (1977)..13
Wise After The Event (1978)..23
Private Parts & Pieces (1979) 31
Sides (1979) 37
Private Parts & Pieces II: Back To The Pavilion (1980)...............................45
1984 (1981) 53
Private Parts & Pieces III: Antiques 59
Invisible Men (1983) 64
Private Parts & Pieces IV: A Catch At The Tables (1984) 76
Private Parts & Pieces V: Twelve (1985) 82
Private Parts & Pieces VI: Ivory Moon 87
Private Parts & Pieces VII: Slow Waves, Soft Stars (1987) 92
Tarka (1988) 99
Missing Links Volume 1: Finger Painting (1989) 103
Slow Dance (1990) 108
Archive Collection Volume I..114
Archive Collection Volume II...124
The Masquerade Tapes 132
Afterword 137

Introduction

Born on 23 December 1951, Anthony Phillips spent his earliest years growing up in the London Borough of Putney until he was packed off to prep school at eight years old. To be suddenly marooned at St Edmunds School, located at Hindhead, in the depths of rural Surrey and far from his parents seemed, to the quiet youngster, a draconian experience to endure. Ant has compared it to being stuck in a horror movie or a POW camp! However, with impressive resolve, he soon buckled down and dug deep to survive this daunting childhood experience. Music only became a passion to him with the advent of The Beatles, at which point he took to the guitar with gusto, inspired by The Shadows' guitarist Hank Marvin. Thankfully, Ant's parents were fully supportive of his musical ambitions, ensuring that he was soon equipped with a Fender Stratocaster electric guitar and a Vox AC30 amplifier, gear of this quality being a rare thing for a soon-to-be-teen back in those days! He also undertook a series of lessons on guitar basics from another of his early musical heroes, classical guitarist Dave Channon. With his new school buddy, Rivers Job (whose surname was pronounced as *Jobe*), who was already the proud owner of a Fender Precision bass guitar, Ant formed his first band, which came together in 1964 and rejoiced under the name of The Spiders. Copying Beatles tunes provided a good musical grounding for the young band.

Later that year, Rivers Job was relocated to Charterhouse Public School near Godalming, a town situated 11 miles northeast of Hindhead on the A3. At 13 years old, Ant followed suit, being inducted into Charterhouse in April 1965 to be once again reunited with his bass-playing pal. The pair of them soon became part of a new band, The Anon, along with Rob Tyrell on drums and Richard Macphail on vocals. This new outfit were also soon joined by Charterhouse rebel Mike Rutherford, initially playing rhythm guitar on a Rickenbacker six-string borrowed from school friend John Alexander. The first significant gig for The Anon took place on Thursday 16 December 1965 at the Charterhouse 'School Entertainment' multi-media event, held in the school hall. With seven bands on the bill, The Anon only had a three-song set, showing a heavy reliance on The Rolling Stones' *Out Of Our Heads* album. Shortly before the curtain was due to go up, a potential disaster was narrowly averted when it transpired that Mike Rutherford had no guitar lead and a mad scramble ensued to furnish him with one before the curtain rose. Happily, The Anon duly dispatched an enthusiastic set, consisting of 'We've Got A Good Thing Going', Chuck Berry's 'Talkin' 'Bout You' and the well-covered deep soul classic 'That's How Strong My Love Is', all previously covered by The Rolling Stones. Meanwhile, Ant was having a bash at writing his own songs, and in the spring of 1966, The Anon decided to record a demo of Ant's new song, 'Pennsylvania Flickhouse'. This demo would see the light of day 56 years later when Esoteric Records issued the Anthony Phillips compilation *The Archive Collection Volume I & Volume II* in 2022 (see later chapter). For the demo session, the band cajoled Ant's mum into transporting their gear in her Mercedes while the band travelled by bus to record at Tony Pike Sound Studios in Dryburgh Road, Putney.

The Charterhouse end-of-term concert in July 1966 proved to be a watershed moment for Ant when The Anon performed with fellow Charterhouse band, The Garden Wall. This latter aggregation included older pupils Peter Gabriel on vocals and Tony Banks on piano, along with trumpeter Johnny Trapman and drummer Chris Stewart. To bolster up their sound, The Garden Wall, who were performing first, invited Ant on guitar and Rivers Job on bass to join them for the set. The Anon, who were headlining the school concert, followed next and started off well with covers of The Beatles' 'Drive My Car' and The Yardbirds' 'Mister, You're A Better Man Than I' before encountering a technical issue which, while it was being corrected, resulted in Richard Macphail making a stage announcement to introduce Ant's latest song, the recently demoed 'Pennsylvania Flickhouse'. However, stage announcements had been forbidden by House Master Geoffrey Ford, who pulled the plug on the concert following the band's rendition of Ant's song. Charterhouse school rules were generally harsh and were strictly adhered to under the threat of physical punishment. This, however, didn't deter the future members of Genesis from periodically sneaking off to Record Corner in the nearby town of Godalming to check out the latest hot sounds!

By the end of the year, The Anon petered out as Phillips and Rutherford became a songwriting collective with Gabriel and Banks. With the inclusion of Chis Stewart on drums, this aggregation would later be christened Genesis. Brian Roberts was a boffin friend of the nascent band, and he invited them to his homemade studio in Chiswick, West London, to record some demos. The first session took place on 26 March 1967 when they recorded, among others, a composition of Ant's called 'Patricia', an instrumental melody which would later be rewritten to appear on the first Genesis album as 'In Hiding'. Further demos were completed by May 1967, and these were touted to Charterhouse 'old boy' Jonathan King during the summer months. Luckily for them, he showed interest, mainly because he loved Peter Gabriel's voice. This led to him booking the band into Regent Sound A Studios in London in December 1967 to record the Banks/Gabriel song 'The Silent Sun', a purposeful nod to the style of King favourites The Bee Gees. He also named the band Genesis, and the first single under this name, 'The Silent Sun' b/w 'That's Me', was released by Decca on 22 February 1968. Both tracks were credited to Genesis, although the B-side, 'That's Me', was a Phillips/Rutherford composition with a prominent electric guitar contribution from Ant. Although the single wasn't hugely successful, King had booked Genesis back into Regent Sound A Studios by May 1968 to record a follow-up disc, and 'A Winter's Tale' b/w 'One-Eyed Hound' was released on 10 May 1968 to a blank reaction from the public. Undeterred, by August 1968, King had the band ensconced in Regent Sound B Studios – with a new drummer in the shape of John Silver – as they recorded their debut album, *From Genesis To Revelation,* in three days. The band were disappointed when they heard the final mix, as King had ordered it to be smothered in cloying string arrangements. Ant hit the roof over this and was embittered by this early experience of the machinations of the music business. The album finally emerged in March 1969 to very poor sales, but the band resolved to carry on and progress.

After regathering themselves, they concentrated on rehearsing and refining a more sophisticated style of music inspired by the advent of King Crimson's iconic 1969 album *In The Court Of The Crimson King.* Ex-lead singer of The Anon, Richard Macphail, became the band's faithful road manager as they sought live gigs going forward. Macphail's parents allowed the band to live and rehearse at Christmas Cottage near Dorking in Surrey and it was here that the unit began to gel and produce some exceptional music. Ant and Mike had started to experiment by combining two 12-string guitars and playing picked chord arpeggios in different inversions. This meshing of 12-strings became a signature sound of early Genesis, which the band would carry forward after Ant had left them. Macphail also provided them with a much-needed bandwagon, a distinctive blue and white Hovis van, to transport the gear to and from their live gigs, which were slowly increasing in number. This formative period at Christmas Cottage, from November 1969 to April 1970, saw the evolution of much new material, and having secured a deal with Charisma Records – via producer John Anthony, who recommended them to Charisma boss Tony Stratton-Smith – the future looked promising.

Ant, however, was quietly having a meltdown. Firstly, his health began to deteriorate, and secondly, he began to encounter intense stage fright, which froze him up, making performing live an unbearable ordeal. Gamely, he held on until the band had completed sessions for their second album at Trident Studios in Soho, London, during June and July 1970 despite him suffering a bout of bronchial pneumonia, but the end was nigh. Immediately after completing the album, he informed a shell-shocked band that he was leaving, which he duly proceeded to do after his last Genesis gig at Sussex Hall, Hayward's Heath, on 18 July 1970. The new Genesis album, *Trespass,* was released in October 1970 on Charisma Records, by which time Ant was considering studying music more seriously and learning classical guitar.

Trespass was a testament to Ant's influence on the Genesis sound, especially his 12-string adventures with his old writing partner Mike Rutherford. This influence would carry forward into the band's classic string of early 1970s albums as they built on the legacy of Ant's contribution. Genesis' follow-up to *Trespass,* 1971's *Nursery Cryme,* had several major tracks, later regarded as Genesis classics by the band's fanbase, that incorporated some of Ant's earlier compositional ideas. Both 'The Musical Box' and 'The Fountain Of Salmacis' deployed themes originally penned by the Phillips/Rutherford team. The first half of 'The Musical Box' was entirely based on an earlier composition called 'F#', penned by the duo in 1969. Some of the themes from 'F#' were recorded by Genesis at BBC Studios in Shepherds Bush on 9 January 1970, as part of a track called 'Manipulation'. This track, along with three others – 'Provocation', 'Frustration' and 'Resignation' – were laid down for a planned BBC documentary on artist Mick Jackson. At the time, Jackson was considered controversial for his sexually-charged imagery depicting S&M themes. The original 1969 demo of 'F#' later appeared on the Phillips compilation album *The Archive Collection Volume I*, which was released in 1998. Going forward, Ant would continue his writing partnership with ex-Anon and Genesis bandmate Mike Rutherford as the duo continued to expand on the twin 12-string template. This would eventually lead to Ant's first solo album, *The Geese & The Ghost*, seeing the light of day, but not before having to overcome countless obstacles scattered over the following six and a half years.

The Geese & The Ghost (1977)

Personnel:

Anthony Phillips: acoustic 12-string, six-string and classical guitar, electric six- and 12-string guitars, basses, dulcimer guitar, bazouki, synthesisers, Mellotron, harmonium, piano, organ, celeste, pin piano, drums, glockenspiel, timbales, bells & chimes, gong, vocals ('Collections')

Mike Rutherford: acoustic 12-string, 6-string and classical guitar, electric six- and 12-string guitars, basses, organ, drums, timbales, glockenspiel, cymbals, bells

Phil Collins: vocals ('Which Way The Wind Blows', 'God If I Saw Her Now', 'Silver Song'), drums ('Silver Song', 'Only Your Love')

Rob Phillips: oboes ('The Geese & The Ghost', 'Sleepfall: The Geese Fly West')

Lazo Momulovich: oboes, cor anglais ('Henry', 'The Geese & The Ghost')

John Hackett: flutes ('God If I Saw Her Now', 'Collections', 'Sleepfall: The Geese Fly West')

Wil Sleath: flute, baroque flute, recorders, piccolo ('Henry')

Jack Lancaster: flutes, lyricon ('Sleepfall: The Geese Fly West')

Charlie Martin: cello ('Chinese Mushroom Cloud', 'The Geese & The Ghost')

Kirk Trevor: cello ('Chinese Mushroom Cloud', 'The Geese & The Ghost')

Nick Hayley: violin ('The Geese & The Ghost')

Martin Westlake: timpani ('Henry', 'Chinese Mushroom Cloud', 'The Geese & The Ghost')

Tom Newman: Hecklephone and bulk eraser

Viv McCauliffe: vocals ('God If I Saw Her Now')

Send Barns Orchestra and Barge Rabble conducted by Jeremy Gilbert

Ralph Bernascone: soloist

David Thomas: classical guitar ('Master Of Time')

Ronnie Gunn: harmonium ('Master Of Time')

Recorded: Send Barns Studios; Argonaut Galleries

Date: 1973-1977

Produced and engineered by Simon Heyworth, Mike Rutherford and Anthony Phillips

Remixed and completed at Trident and Olympic Studios (engineer: Anton Matthews)

Cover artwork: Peter Cross

Record label: Hit & Run (UK), Passport (US)

Released: March 1977, Hit & Run; CD rerelease, Virgin 1990; two-disc rerelease, Voiceprint 2008; three-disc definitive edition CD rerelease, Esoteric 2015

Within ten days of quitting Genesis in July 1970, Ant had demoed much of the material that would eventually constitute his debut solo album, *The Geese & The Ghost*. He then pursued his dream of embarking on more advanced musical study by enrolling at The Guildhall School of Music & Drama in London. The material for his first solo effort, therefore, remained on the shelf until spring 1972, when, along with cohort Mike Rutherford, he began to map an outline for an album project. As Rutherford had pressing commitments with Genesis, work was slotted in when gaps appeared in the busy Genesis schedule.

Tony Stratton-Smith of Charisma Records stumped up the cash to record a potential single of Ant's composition, 'Silver Song', written back in 1969 as a farewell to Genesis' departing drummer, John Silver. Interestingly, it was the concurrent Genesis drummer Phil Collins who would end up providing the vocals for this track. So Ant was booked into Island Studios in Basing Street, London, in November 1973, along with Mike Rutherford and Phil Collins, to record 'Silver Song', plus a B-side with hastily written lyrics entitled 'Only Your Love'. Charisma then got cold feet, and the single didn't see the light of day. Happily, both sides of this recording were included as bonus tracks on Esoteric Records' definitive edition of *The Geese & The Ghost* in 2015.

However, Charisma did come through with a release for Ant and Mike's attempt at a modern hymn in the shape of a song called 'Take This Heart'. This was a choral composition performed by the Charterhouse Choral Society at Charterhouse Chapel and accompanied by organist Robin Wells. The live recording of it was captured by Brian Roberts, who had previously helped Genesis record demos back in their early days. The recording appeared on the album *Beyond An Empty Dream*, released by Charisma Records in April 1975. The 1972 demo of this song later appeared on the Blueprint Records two-CD set *Archive Collection Volume I*.

In the summer of 1974, Charisma advanced £3,000 towards Ant's new project and this supplied two TEAC four-track tape machines and a mixing desk on which work could now proceed at Send Barns near Woking, Surrey – a facility on the premises of Ant's parents' place and an ongoing recording venue for him through the next nine years. October 1974 saw Ant and Mike progressing well as they built up the basic tracks; then, with Mike away on Genesis' *The Lamb Lies Down On Broadway* tour between 26 November and 5 December, Ant pressed on with fleshing out the proposed material for the new album.

April 1975 saw further sessions at Send Barns, where ex-Genesis roadie David Rootes provided invaluable assistance to Ant as they built up the basic tracks for the new album prior to a move to Argonaut Galleries, Tom Newman's recording facility on a barge moored on the canals of Little Venice in Maida Vale, London. By this stage, Argonaut engineer Simon Heyworth had helped to shape the new recordings with his production skills, as his encouragement kept Ant believing that this new project would eventually see the light of day. Another setback came when Charisma decided against releasing *The Geese & The Ghost,* but luckily, Ant's manager, Tony Smith, arranged for his company Hit & Run to release the album in the UK, while Passport Records covered its release in the US.

Later, in 1975, after Peter Gabriel had left Genesis, their former frontman called on some old mates to help him demo a bunch of new songs. Ant, Mike

Rutherford and Phil Collins assisted Gabriel in recording early versions of songs that would make up his debut solo album, which would later be recorded in America with producer Bob Ezrin and released around the time of Ant's solo debut in early 1977.

Another project that Ant became involved in whilst on a trip to the US around this time was an album put together by songwriter Wil Malone and producers Stephen Galfas and Marty Scott. This project was known as the Intergalactic Touring Band and Ant was featured playing acoustic guitar on the track 'Reaching Out', with vocals by Annie Haslam of Renaissance. The album was released in the US on Passport Records on 15 October 1977, with a UK release on Charisma Records following a month later.

The cover artwork for *The Geese & The Ghost* was provided by talented artist Peter Cross and is eye-catchingly gorgeous. A medieval minstrel sits on a grassy slope with his lute, overlooking a verdant valley with a lake, as a ghostly figure appears to arise from the water. It's one of those covers you could scrutinise for ages, containing many tiny details to amuse and delight. The rear of the sleeve sports the credits, alongside further amusing Peter Cross artwork showing a goose wearing an armoured helmet while sundry other high-flying birds attempt to bomb the armoured fowl from the sky. Cross would continue to provide artwork for many of Ant's albums going forward, most of them feeling symbiotically part of the artistic statement of each album.

When *The Geese & The Ghost* finally appeared in March 1977, it was embraced by many Genesis fans, although, sadly, some general press reviews were coloured by the bias at the time towards the more stripped-down sounds of the punk movement. Unfortunately, these reviewers evinced a sense of ennui towards the intricacies of the progressive rock style that had so dominated the early 1970s musical landscape.

'Wind – Tales' (Phillips)

This ambient introductory track floats in on a stiff breeze, sounding as if it's built on part of a recording running backwards, possibly with tape-reversed orchestration mixed in. It fades out after just over a minute, nicely setting up the first song of this set, which also uses the wind as a metaphor.

'Which Way The Wind Blows' (Phillips)

Originally demoed in July 1970, this was the first piece to be committed to *The Geese & The Ghost* sessions when, in October 1974, Ant, along with Mike Rutherford, laid down the twin 12-string guitar parts that would form the basis of this charming, folk-flavoured song. With its delicate 12-string guitar structure, you could well imagine it being performed by the medieval minstrel of the cover artwork as he sits overlooking a pastoral scene while ruminating on the capricious winds of change that delineate human fortunes. Strongly folk-flavoured, it feels as if it could have been minted in centuries past, such is its timeless flavour. Phil Collins does a sterling job in the vocal department; his voice is panned to one side of the stereo picture, with occasional double-tracking of harmony vocals panned to the opposite speaker at judicious points in the proceedings.

The delicate web of 12-string guitars is an obvious continuation and development of the Phillips/Rutherford 12-string work of their early Genesis recordings. Although mostly 12-string, there are some mandolin and harp-like tones in the filigree web of gentle acoustic sound that constitutes the matrix of this song. Some discreet electric guitar lines are added at one point, but the intricate feel is always retained. The choruses revert to chord strumming as Collins' vocals paint a vivid portrait of the protagonist of the song peacefully observing the setting sun, only to then be disturbed by the uncertain thought of which way the metaphorical wind will blow the tides of fortune, as his future unfolds. There is a section of guitar picking towards the end of the song that will recur towards the close of side one on the track 'God If I Saw Her Now', tying together the two songs of the first side. On 'Which Way The Wind Blows', this section builds as the track nears its end, supported by swelling organ chords, before fading out on some tinkling musical box-like guitar picking.

'Henry: Portraits From Tudor Times' (Phillips, Rutherford)

On the original vinyl LP, this track was divided into six parts, although the 2015 Esoteric definitive edition remaster features an added section in the form of a reprise of the second part: 'Lute's Chorus'. First conceived and demoed in July 1970, the composition expanded in scope between then and its final form on *The Geese & The Ghost* in 1977. The music conjures a series of impressions of preparation for, and the aftermath of, The Battle of the Spurs, part of a war waged between England and France in 1513, the English contingent being led by Henry VIII and his army.

The first part, 'Fanfare', represents the opening of the court of King Henry VIII, evoking lavish pageantry and splendour. A rolling figure played on organ fades up to a staccato keyboard fanfare, laced with liberal doses of reverb, making it sound like the event is unfolding in a huge stone hall. After 56 seconds, the opening fanfare gives way to a second section, the charmingly authentic 'Lute's Chorus', with its madrigal-like ambience and gentle acoustic arpeggios. When joined by the piping recorders and baroque flute of Wil Neath, the sound recalls that of those early 1970s medieval pranksters, Gryphon. 'Lute's Chorus' represents lavish feasting in the Long Hall, over which the Master of the Revels presides.

The third section, 'Misty Battlements', is a more poignant interlude with gentle guitar picking that falls into a triple-time strum, evoking dawn breaking over Gloucester Castle as knights gaze into the misty vista with a mixture of unease and excitement as war with France beckons. In many ways, the overall structure of 'Henry' recalls side two of King Crimson's 1970 album

Lizard (but minus the jazz element), as it follows a similar sequence of events (preparation, battle and aftermath), albeit from a more historical perspective than *Lizard*'s more mythical feel. 'Misty Battlements' was written by Ant during a holiday in Ireland with Mike Rutherford in 1973.

Part four, 'Henry Goes To War', depicts the English fleet assembling, followed by invasion and The Battle of the Spurs. High drama is invoked via staccato, rhythmically-aggressive electric guitar strokes as the woodwind section join in with gusto. The dynamic dips in the music create a vision of skirmishes and lulls in the action prior to one final thrust, in which the drums and cymbals join the throng and the electric guitar gets more abrasive, depicting the white heat of battle. This section has a very 'live' feel, as it decelerates and speeds up organically, reflecting the natural flow of the battle it's portraying.

After the devastation of battle comes the inevitable lament. It makes up the fifth section of 'Henry' and is entitled 'Death Of A Knight'. A conceptual equivalent to 'Prince Rupert's Lament' from King Crimson's *Lizard*, this mournful elegy returns to triple time for its poignant guitar-picked melody.

The final section of 'Henry' sees the opening fanfare return, this time punctuated by three timpani booms, sounding like celebratory cannons as the victorious king returns. Recording the timpani caused a good deal of bother, as by the time 'Triumphant Return' was recorded, the whole ensemble had moved onto The Argonaut barge, moored in Little Venice, Maida Vale. The problem was that the timpani were too bulky to get on board the barge, so a solution was proposed whereby they were located on a larger neighbouring barge and piped through to The Argonaut, where Simon Heyworth captured the sound on tape. The results proved well worth the effort as a church organ and a hastily organised bunch of volunteers, dubbed Barge Rabble, transform the sequence from the previous 'Lute's Chorus' section by performing an uplifting chorale to end proceedings in a celebratory fashion. One big organ chord marks the end of the 'Henry' saga. With its programmatic thrust, it's a piece that points the way towards Ant's future employment as a provider of film and library music, which started as a sideline but eventually became his most reliable source of income.

'God If I Saw Her Now' (Phillips)

Another song originating from Ant's July 1970 demo sessions, this plaintive ballad was designed as a male/female duet of mainly alternating verses. The basic track for this recording was laid down by Ant at Send Barns between 26 November and 5 December 1974 while Mike Rutherford was away on Genesis' *The Lamb Lies Down On Broadway* tour. Originally sporting a solo on his Fender Stratocaster electric guitar, this was later superseded by John Hackett's fluttering flute solo on the final version. Phil Collins makes his second cameo appearance on the album as he shares vocal duties with Viv McAuliffe (ex-Principal Edwards Magic Theatre). Incidentally, Principal

Edwards are a band well worth checking out for fans of early 1970s progressive rock. By the time I became enamoured by their music in 1973, Viv McCauliffe had left them, but in a live setting, the slimmed-down lineup proved to be dynamite. The band recorded the excellent 1974 album *Round One*, produced by Pink Floyd drummer Nick Mason.

The combination of Collins and McAuliffe here works well, enhancing this folk-tinged ode, which looks back on an earlier love affair and those unique feelings conjured by a special first love.

Accompanied by gentle guitar picking, Viv McAuliffe takes the first verse, wondering what her resting partner is thinking about. In verse two, Phil Collins sings tenderly that he is thinking of his first love, causing his female partner to question if he loved this early sweetheart more than he loves her, to which he remains non-committal, waxing eloquently about that earlier, more innocent love affair, to which she finally concludes: 'You loved her more than me'. The male protagonist admits that he was jilted by his earlier lover and the song ends with a statement of its title. Prior to this last verse, the arpeggio picking section from 'Which Way The Wind Blows', referred to earlier, reoccurs here, nicely tying together the two songs of side one that provide the sliced bread of a tasty musical sandwich, with the filling being the more epic 'Henry' suite.

'Chinese Mushroom Cloud' (Phillips, Rutherford)
Side two opens with chiming 12-string guitars, sounding akin to a startled flock of geese taking flight, as dramatic cello and electric guitar crash in, mirroring the ominous portent enshrined in the title of this short but potent opening piece. It's a theme that will be more fully developed in the two-part album title track which follows.

'The Geese & The Ghost (Parts 1 & 2)' (Phillips, Rutherford)
If side one of *The Geese & The Ghost* acted as an aperitif, then side two is the main course of the heartily nourishing musical banquet that makes up this album. Evolving from a 1969 Phillips/Rutherford composition, then known as 'D Instrumental', the title track opens with Ant and Mike's twin 12-string guitars slowly and patiently constructing another of their intricate webs of crystalline sound to form the matrix for the track's slow orchestral build. This delicate twin guitar web was recorded at Send Barns in October 1974. The title for this piece was inspired by two sounds discovered by Ant whilst experimenting with his ARP Pro-soloist synthesiser. The 'geese' are represented by a repeated, rolling note sequence that strongly evokes a high-flying flock of birds, while the 'ghost' is portrayed by a more spectral-like upward synthesiser glissando, both of which will reoccur later in the piece. The initial 12-string theme is soon picked up by Ant's gentle celeste as some guitar harmonics also flicker in. As the theme builds, piano joins the fray and a horn introduces the next thematic development of this gently evolving piece.

A three-note motif moves through several modulations before the bass guitar and drumkit are introduced, giving the track a forward motion that suggests the earthbound birds of the title are preparing to take flight until an upward piano run peters out, momentarily bringing them back to earth once more.

Some glockenspiel tinkles precede another slow build on the initial theme again as the ARP 'geese' make their first appearance around 4.40 and the debut of the ARP 'ghost' follows shortly thereafter. As the track builds once more, the dancing woodwind and piano invoke tinkling waterfalls before the three-note motif returns once more to reinstate a slow build. This section features a richly harmonic blend of oboe and flute that Ant jokingly dubbed 'floboe' at the time. It's a gorgeously warm sound and the simplicity of the three-note motif lends the track an impressive sense of space. The piping woodwind section bubbles around underneath and the piece proceeds towards its second climax. First, a pulsing bass drum enters, along with John Hackett's fluttering flute, then the full drumkit, plus cymbals crashing in, as an upward synthesiser glissando and big organ chord find the geese of the title airborne once more, bringing part one of the title track to a close.

Part two opens with some mysterious tones fading in and then out again several times before the chiming guitar we previously encountered in 'Chinese Mushroom Cloud' appears, along with the dramatic theme from that track. An electric guitar melody develops this theme into a more convoluted riff that literally takes flight, like the birds of the title, with the track becoming more dynamic, with impressive timpani work enhancing a relentless build-up. The ascent to the climax of this section forms a tension that is released in a wonderful drop into a floating, violin-led passage that feels like a hang-glider cresting a ridge with an elating release into the air – suddenly, it feels as if we're flying along with the geese!

Following this glorious interlude, the music falls back to some heavily phased 12-string guitar strums, initiating a third return towards the big crescendo that closed the first part of the track, where the drums and bass kick in to punctuate the build-up as they relentlessly ascend towards a glorious Mellotron string chord climax, with the Mellotron's choral tapes providing a fading afterglow.

A more poignant cor anglais-led theme brings a hint of sadness to the music prior to the rhythmic coda. This endpiece fades in on gentle guitar strumming over a circular-sounding sequence. Here, Ant cleverly builds several of the themes, including the elaborate guitar riffing heard earlier, supported by a shuffling bass and drum rhythm. Eventually, all fades away in this rhythmic closing section, completing a track that evinces a very classical feel and is blessed with a superb arrangement.

'Collections' (Phillips)
Another song of 1969 vintage, 'Collections' was demoed at Send Barns in Spring 1974, along with 'Autumnal', a piano piece that ended up on the later

Private Parts & Pieces. An orchestrated version of the latter was originally scheduled for *The Geese & The Ghost* but was left off the final master at Charisma's behest. This version of 'Collections' was recorded at Olympic Studios, London, during the final sessions for the album. Ant's piano backing is beautifully decorated by his brother Rob's plaintive oboe and the flutes of John Hackett and Jack Lancaster (the latter, ex-Blodwyn Pig).

Lyrically, the song consists of a series of philosophical reflections posed over a succession of four verses. It reflects on vulnerability: the balance between the weak and the strong; the predator and the prey; and compassion, or the lack of it. It's true to say that Ant is probably more strongly associated with instrumental compositions rather than songwriting, but I, for one, am a massive fan of 'Ant the Songwriter', and thankfully, there is a decent-sized canon of Ant's songs peppered throughout his predominantly instrumental output over the years.

'Sleepfall: The Geese Fly West' (Phillips)

The same team that recorded 'Collections' provide a quintessential ending to this beautiful album, with one of the simplest but most perfect pieces on this collection. Ant recorded his piano part at Send Barns in October 1976 and the woodwind overdubs were added at Olympic Studios the following month. It consists of a repeated and quite intoxicating piano sequence, successively overlaid with a gorgeous orchestral build via Rob Phillips' oboe, John Hackett's pastoral flute and Jack Lancaster's Lyricon, a 1970s wind synthesiser. 'Sleepfall' engenders a feeling of peace in its gently reflective way and with the sun setting on Ant's first solo venture, he manipulates his ARP Pro-soloist synthesizer to conjure the vision of a skein of geese flying into a blissfully perfect sunset.

Additional Material
'Master Of Time' (Phillips)

This demo was included on the Virgin 1990 rerelease and disc two of the 2015 Esoteric definitive edition of the album. Recorded at Send Barns in August 1973, it features Ant on guitar, David Thomas on classical guitar and Ronnie Gunn on piano and harmonium. Originally intended for inclusion on *The Geese & The Ghost*, it's a wonderful song, charmingly sung by Ant in that fragile way that is solely his. I'm a big fan of Phillips' voice; he seems to engender a subtle emotion in his vocal performances and, once combined with the yearning lyrics here, is full of feeling. The lyrics cover similar territory to the later Steve Hackett song 'Turn Back Time' (from the 1981 album *Cured*), where the protagonist longs for a second chance to relive the passage of the years once more to hopefully strive towards being more giving. But, alas, the arrow of time points only one way for us mere mortals, rendering such wishes an impossible dream. It does make for a movingly poignant song, which would, 37 years after this recording, be covered by progressive rock band Big Big Train on the first issue of their 2010 mini-album *Far Skies, Deep Time*.

Ant's demo is kept simple and opens with acoustic guitar picking, quickly joined by a gently strumming 12-string guitar. The choruses turn to a more insistent strum as Ant beseeches the 'Master of Time' to take him back through the years. Ronnie Gunn's fluid piano cascades appear as the second verse commences. Following a further chorus, a harmonium chord pad announces the lengthy coda on which the trio initiate a jam over a couple of repeated chords. This lengthens this simple song to an extended 7.37, but the trio are obviously enjoying themselves on this end section, with Gunn getting well carried away with his swirling piano triplets, as well as overdubbing additional harmonium chords as the song fades. All in all, it proves to be a welcome addition to the material on the original album.

'Silver Song' (Phillips, Rutherford)
This 1969 tribute to the then-departing Genesis percussionist John Silver is, in many ways, a typical Phillips/Rutherford Genesis song from their early period. Simple and catchy, the chorus refrain easily lodges in the brain, and the whole thing, both verse and chorus, is built over the same sequence in a home key of G. It's the movement from the verse to the chord progression Dm-Am-Em-A-D that turns it around and gives the tune its irresistible lilt – it's quite an addictive sequence actually! This proposed single version is the 1973 recording by the trio of Ant on guitars and keys, Mike Rutherford on bass and Phil Collins on drums and vocals. It's a shame Charisma pulled it as a single back then, as it may have even crept chart-wards, with Genesis on an upward curve in popularity at the time. As you would expect, the Genesis rhythm section give this something special, as Rutherford's bass and Collins' drums lock into a snaking fluidity of motion that drives the track forward admirably. Ant adds some subtle electric guitar decoration in the middle section and provides the playful Moog contribution that dances over Collins' passionate vocals as the track fades – quite delicious!

'Only Your Love' (Phillips, Rutherford)
The proposed single required a B-side, so Ant revived an idea he'd had the previous year. A short writing session with Mike Rutherford furnished some rudimentary lyrics before 'Only Your Love' was committed to tape at Island Studios, London, in November 1973. Built around a D chord, the song was even simpler than its proposed A-side but was given an enthusiastic performance by the trio. Again, it's the Rutherford/Collins rhythm section that provide the most interesting musical aspect here. Very much B-side material, Collins gives his usual 100% commitment in the vocal department and the song is hung on its wordless chorus as Collins chants a nonsensical 'Nye-nye-nye-nye-nye' refrain. Again, this rare vintage track was a welcome addition to the collection for Ant and Genesis fans when it finally appeared on disc two of the Esoteric definitive edition remaster of *The Geese & The Ghost* in 2015.

'Lines In The Sand' (Phillips, Rootes)

Recorded at Send Barns at the April 1975 sessions, where Ant, in conjunction with former Genesis roadie David Rootes, was struggling towards completing potential material for his first solo outing, *The Geese & The Ghost*. It's a heavily experimental piece with Ant on piano and David Rootes manipulating the graphic equalizer. Built around two vacillating piano notes and some slight chordal movements, bouncing to-and-fro, the result is a hypnotic see-sawing effect with subtle variations of timbre as Rootes manipulates the EQ. This experiment was in aid of potential overdubs to the tracks on *The Geese & The Ghost*, but this recording only became available on the CD *Private Parts & Extra Pieces*, released in 2015 as part of the Esoteric Records box set *Private Parts & Pieces I-IV*.

'Still-Born Love' (Phillips)

This piano-based piece, composed in 1972, was recorded at Send Barns in the summer of 1977 and provided the closing track to the *Private Parts & Extra Pieces* CD. It's a track that was worth waiting for, though, running for a duration of 9.20.

Opening with tinkling piano notes, it moves into a descending sequence with flurries of high runs. Around 1.14, some very deep notes rebound as cascading arpeggios of dancing piano notes circle above. There's an impressive upward run on the keys between 2.18 and 2.23 before the piece moves to a slower, more thoughtful contemplation thereafter. The piece is built on a very song-like structure with a strong chord progression. Some very high runs around the four-minute mark contrast with dramatic deep stalking notes, and around 4.48, the tinkling variations conjure the vision of a musical box or perhaps a dancing ballerina. The big upward run on the keys returns between 7.36 and 7.41, ushering in a slower-sounding, contemplative drift. The whole piece displays a strong underlying emotional feel. Apart from the piano that dominates, there are occasional, subtle harmonium overdubs added in the background.

Wise After The Event (1978)

Personnel:
Anthony Phillips: vocals, harmonium
Michael Giles: drums
John G. Perry: Wal custom bass
The Vicar: guitars, keyboards, sundries
Jeremy Gilbert: keyboards ('Greenhouse'), harp ('Now What')
Mel Collins: soprano sax ('We're All As We Lie'), flutes ('Birdsong', 'Tremulous')
Robin Phillips: oboe ('Sitars & Nebulous')
Rupert Hine: percussion, backing vocals, vibes
Perkin Alanbeck: synthesiser ('Birdsong')
Humbert Ruse and Vic Stench: drums, bass ('Greenhouse')
Rodent Rabble: clicks, claps
Orchestra on 'Regrets' assembled by David Katz, arranged by Anthony Phillips and conducted by Gilbert Biberian
Recorded: Essex Studios (October 1977); Manor Mobile at 'The Farmyard' (November/December 1977); CBS Studios (December 1977)
Engineer: Richard 'Papercup' Austen (Essex); Alan Perkins (Manor Mobile); Steve Taylor (CBS); mixed at Trident Studios by Peter Kelsey (December 1977 – January 1978)
Producer: Rupert Hine
Cover artwork: Peter Cross
Record label: Arista (UK); Passport (US)
Released: 12 May 1978, Arista; CD rerelease, Virgin 1990; CD rerelease, Voiceprint 2008; four-disc definitive edition CD rerelease, Esoteric 2016

In many ways, it's a shame that Ant failed to get his debut album released until 1977, as the late-1970s scene, in general, was less conducive to the kind of musical subtlety that was his forte. He soldiered on regardless and the 1977 to 1978 period found him busying himself recording a second album project. This time, he'd managed to build another solid team of musicians to work with, particularly the crack rhythm section of bassist John G Perry (ex-Caravan and Quantum Jump) and ex-King Crimson drummer and noted eccentric Mike Giles. Another plus for Ant was the production nous of ex-Quantum Jump vocalist/keyboardist Rupert Hine, who joined the team as producer for the next two of Ant's mainstream albums: *Wise After The Event* and *Sides*.

Sessions for the first of these albums were initiated at Essex Studios in October 1977 before moving on to The Farmyard, Buckinghamshire, with assistance from The Manor Mobile Studio, over the remainder of 1977. Following orchestral overdubs at CBS Studios in December 1977, Ant returned to Trident Studios in Soho, London (where, eight years earlier, he had been recording *Trespass* with Genesis) to mix the album with engineer Peter Kelsey, completing the project by January 1978.

The marvellous and wonderfully surreal cover artwork was again provided by Peter Cross, with illustrations of sundry animal life, including a teched-up bionic red squirrel, apparently loitering on the moon in the hope of a game of cosmic golf! All the illustrations were inspired by the idiosyncratic content of Ant's new collection of songs housed within Cross's handsome sleeve. The credits are peppered with Ant's oblique sense of humour and, along with a listing of the musicians involved, they are peopled with unlikely characters such as Ralph Bernascone, Vic Stench and The Vicar (the last two of these, seemingly, are pseudonyms for Ant himself!). These personalities and many more will recur on many of his releases going forward. The credits also list several tracks that don't appear on the album, as the cover artwork was completed before the final master was finished and some of the shorter linking tracks were removed at the last minute. As the artwork was so elaborate, the decision was made to go with it. Happily, many of the lost links would turn up via Ant's *Private Parts & Pieces* series of albums going forward.

Again, press notices were generally critical of the album content, unfairly in my view, as this album gave vent to the wild imagination of 'Ant the songwriter'. Eccentric ditties dominated, rather than Ant's more expansive instrumental adventures, resulting in an album that mixed his oblique humour with more philosophical reflection to produce a potent and imaginative brew to amuse and delight his listeners.

'We're All As We Lie' (Phillips)

The album opens with a solid slice of whimsy, led by a repeating, double-tracked guitar hook over a G major chord, nicely panned to either side of the stereo mix, which, along with a change to D minor for the second half, forms the basis of the verse. An occasional sitar-like drone rises to the surface at regular intervals, while the understated rhythm section of John Perry and Mike Giles tastefully support the groove. Lyrically, we're in cosmic territory as Ant regales the tale of a highly unusual game of golf, apparently played by a succession of animalistic characters. It all ends up on the moon – so far, so surreal!

The title chorus hook, sung over the chords F and C, is rather catchy and hummable, introducing another underlying theme that runs through this album: the acquisition of wisdom ('Getting wiser, so much wiser'). An instrumental break finds the inestimable Mel Collins providing a gorgeous soprano sax solo, which breaks up the song nicely, while The Vicar chips in with some tasty lead guitar decorations on the fadeout over the repeated chorus chords. Although the lyric mentions Apollo 11 astronaut Buzz Aldrin, this song may well have been inspired by astronaut Alan Shepherd's game of lunar golf on 6 February 1971 during NASA's Apollo 14 mission.

'Birdsong' (Phillips)

Written as far back as 1970, 'Birdsong' is introduced by Ant's gently strumming acoustic guitar as he reflects on the natural beauty of the dawn chorus, with its enchanting medley of sound that announces each new spring day. The verses are connected by a swaying bridge, leading into a rising sequence, as some understated electric guitar lines decorate the picture. An upward flourish on piano then signals a return to the gentle strumming of the next verse. A more harp-like sound moves over this second verse/bridge section as an uplifting orchestral sweep enters the picture.

The lyrics conjure picturesque locations with mysterious-sounding names. Mentions of evocative localities, such as Heron's Flood, Cragshorn and Dorn Ridge, fire the listener's imagination, placing the song in an unspecified locale (although there's a Dorn Ridge in New Brunswick, Canada!). Verse three is embellished by some tasteful electric guitar noodling, ending with John Perry unleashing one of his patent bass swoops into a bridge section that sports a more astringent guitar solo by Ant, with some emotive bent notes on display. More reverb is added towards the end of the guitar solo, along with some well-judged tom fills by drummer Mike Giles. The contrast between the quieter and more assertive passages of this recording underlines an impressive grasp of dynamics, emphasising what a tightly drilled unit this new lineup is.

Just when you think the track has ended, an unexpected triple-time coda appears with Mel Collins returning once more to make a tasteful contribution on flute along with Ant's strummed acoustic and gentle vocal as the track fades.

'Moonshooter' (Phillips)

Freshly written for the album, this song returns to a lunar theme, but this time as a metaphor for ambition, summed up by the well-known phrase 'shooting for the moon'. The protagonist of the song appears to be an unnamed female. The lyric is more a series of impressions rather than a fully realised story, as Ant's lyrics remain ambiguous. His voice does carry a good deal of emotion, though, especially on the triple-time choruses, where the vocals emit a curious, fragile, almost crackling sound during the line, 'no gaping *cracks* to hide'. It's a distinctive quirk of his vocalising that is present in a fair few of his songs and transmits a subtle emotion that I've always found quite endearing.

Musically, the verses are gently strummed acoustic affairs, contrasting with the more rhythmic chorus strumming. The chord sequence of the latter bears a distinctive rhythmic and chordal relationship to the verses of his pal Mike Rutherford's song, 'Your Own Special Way', a minor hit single for Genesis in 1977. There are many lovely touches to the arrangement as this song wends its gentle way, including a refined bass contribution from John Perry and some restrained electric guitar doodling and tinkling piano arpeggios from The Vicar himself.

'Wise After The Event' (Phillips)

Clocking in at ten-and-a-half minutes, this is very much the epic track of the album. It starts out enigmatically, with some mysterious tones fading in and out before we run into an imposing wall of rhythmic 12-string guitars moving at a slow and steady tempo. John Perry's pulsing bass line joins in as he plays one throbbing note on each beat. Proceeding like a measured, ultra-slow march, the first verse invites us to follow the fortunes of 'Four thousand monks in a maelstrom' whilst also raising the ghost of doom-mongering soothsayer Old Mother Hailsham. The mood of the piece becomes ever-more ominous, especially when, after a few verses building tension, a contrasting 12-string arpeggio bridge section lifts the tune ever-upwards, with an apocalyptic feel to the music.

The lyrics reinforce this feel, mixing the mythical and the historical by drawing imagery from different eras. Whether the lyric makes any literal sense is debatable, but that doesn't matter, as the overwhelming feeling here is of the heroic, like some lost epic poem – the lyrics fit the music like a glove.

By verse three, Mike Giles' drum kit enters the picture, still with the creeping slowness that amplifies the oracular feel of this piece. It's classic progressive rock territory we're in here as the bridge returns, this time with some subtle percussion effects added to the mix.

For the instrumental middle section of the song, Ant moves his picking hand closer to the bridge of the guitar, creating a spikier arpeggio sound, before embarking on an elaborate 12-string odyssey that displays his mastery of the instrument most associated with him through the years. It's a marvellous passage, ranging wide and free, punctuated by Giles' subtle tom-tom booms with added reverb. In its scope and tone, it shares a kinship with Al Stewart's similarly wide-ranging guitar excursion on 'Nostradamus' from the 1974 album *Past, Present & Future*. Ant's solo eventually concludes with some wobbly-sounding chording before leading back to the song proper for one final verse.

Possibly influenced by the then-recent death of Elvis Presley, the lyrics then take one final surreal turn by evoking the multitudes marching on Memphis to pay their respects to the King of Rock 'n' Roll. The portentous, funereal beat is joined by a rhythmic keyboard effect in this verse. The final repeating chanted punchline to this epic song returns to the theme of accumulating wisdom ('getting so much wiser, it's so much fun'). Some filtered backing vocals echo the chant, buried deep in the mix, as the pulsing track peters out on some 12-string guitar harmonics.

An unexpected coda drifts in, closing side one on an unsettling note. This is actually a 12-string and Polymoog mix of the end section of the final track of side two of the album, 'Now What (Are They Doing To My Little Friends)', conveniently tying both sides of the album together conceptually.

'Pulling Faces' (Phillips)
Side two opens with some low-level plucking sounds, soon falling into a dramatic bass pedal effect intro that mirrors Genesis' then-contemporaneous

sound. Topped with electric guitar riffs, the intro works through some tricky time signatures before settling into a thumping 4/4 bass drum-driven verse. The towering chorus arrives with its ascending sequence, giving the song high drama. It's a track with much beautifully subtle bass work from John Perry, often playing high on the neck of his instrument, including some two-note hammering. The contrast of the straightforward verses with the melodrama of the choruses ensures there are some impressive dynamics on display, underlining what a fabulous unit Ant has employed for this project.

Lyrically, we're back with the cosmic theme and much amusing wordplay on all matters interstellar. The protagonist, whoever they may be, has apparently been exiled out in space, but despite this, they seem to be having fun exploring the outer reaches of our star system, as well as partaking in planetary adventures closer to home. It's all very tongue-in-cheek but right up this listener's cosmic highway! Humour, drama and great music combined, what's not to like?

A build-up of ascending, ever-accelerating riffs on the coda suggests a kind of 'A Day In The Life' moment is approaching, but it never arrives; the song instead finishes on a kind of musical precipice, with just a reverb reflection left. It evokes the feeling of vanishing into a cosmic wormhole – very fitting!

'Regrets' (Phillips)

Featuring the only overtly personal lyric on the album, 'Regrets' is a tender piano ballad written by Ant in 1975. The verses owe an obvious debt to the Jacques Revaux 1967 tune 'Comme D'Habitude', which later became the more familiarly known standard 'My Way', once furnished with English lyrics by Paul Anka. 'Regrets' is not the first song to bear such influence; another prominent example is David Bowie's 'Life On Mars' from his 1971 album *Hunky Dory*. Ant soon puts his own stamp on 'Regrets' though, taking it beyond this initial similarity.

The structure works through a repeated verse/chorus/bridge sequence, all the time building up the arrangement via an increasingly grandiose orchestral arrangement created by Ant himself and conducted by one Gilbert Biberian (possibly a pseudonym for Jeremy Gilbert). There are some lovely touches to the orchestration, especially the flute figures on the bridge, which remind me a bit of the 1950s ballad 'Catch A Falling Star'. Although subtle at first, in some of the later verses, the arrangement becomes a tad 'kitchen sink' with everything thrown in, including some big, descending brass parts that pile on the emotional overkill.

That being said, this is a lovely, poignant song, nailing its subject with some perceptive and touching lines. In the final verse, the notion of regrets as 'our secret cemeteries' where we quietly lay to rest our loves and losses is spot on. Ant genuinely seems to be mourning a lost love here, perhaps the mysterious Lucy, a ballerina that he had obvious feelings for in his younger days and who proved to be the muse for many of his love songs from this period.

'Greenhouse' (Phillips, Gilbert)

Written in 1976 by Ant along with Jeremy Gilbert, here we're back with fanciful eccentricity and also with outer space, as the working title for this song was the less concise 'Sleeping On An Interstellar Plane'. A distinctive synthesiser riff against Ant's guitar forms the intro, leading into another fine band performance as this ditty wends its whimsical way through a verse/chorus structure, with the occasional variation thrown in. What makes this track different from the others on this album is its rhythm section, consisting of Ant on bass and Rupert Hine on drums, billed in the credits as Vic Stench and Humbert Ruse!

Much jocular wordplay is in evidence as we contemplate wind, snow and rain combined with honourable mentions of Sir Francis Drake and his sinking of the Spanish Armada as common sense bows to the surreal. A love of language and puns predominate over meaning in this catchy three-minute ode to who knows what. As the synthesiser riff that brought us in makes a return, we're still none the wiser, but the journey has proved to be a heap of good fun!

'Paperchase' (Phillips)

Next up is one of the finest songs on this album, introducing itself with a short intro displaying a triple-time lilt. Over an acoustic backing strum, Ant performs a series of eight two-note figures on electric guitar, sounding as if he is fretting a note, then wiggling his finger to-and-fro across the fretboard, producing a sound which conjures blossoms spiralling to earth in a gentle spring breeze. After this lovely intro, a gently strummed acoustic guitar with a touch of phasing supports the 4/4 verses. These are linked to the chorus of the song via a bridge that becomes ever more dynamic thanks to the Perry/Giles rhythm section, who sound glued together, such is their distinctive rapport with each other's playing. Perry's bass is soft but very lyrical in the verses. He is also incredibly potent in the bridge sections, where he employs some downward bass swoops – very much a signature of his refined playing style. These bass swoops are treated with liberal doses of reverb by producer Rupert Hine, sounding utterly wonderful in their dynamism. Check out the bass/drum unison figure that leads into the final bridge at 3.36, where Perry's bass and Giles' drum fill sound cements together – it's an awesome moment!

As well as guitars, Ant provides some tinkling piano arpeggios throughout, most especially a feature of the choruses. He also gives a moving vocal performance, imploring the subject of the song to give him a call if they're ever in doubt and he'll 'be right round' – what a lovely fella he is! Written in 1976, the lyrics contain some wonderfully resonant phrases that range from the poignant to the celebratory. The subtitle of the song is 'May Never Wears A Frown', and the bridge sections use the poetic device of anadiplosis: this is where the final word of one line then becomes the first word of the following line, the pivotal word, in this case, being 'May'. It's all clever stuff and adds an extra refined touch to this fascinating slice of classic songwriting.

'Now What (Are They Doing To My Little Friends?)' (Phillips)
A song composed by Ant under the working title 'Hunt Song', it was written after viewing a TV programme about seal culling. It provides a grand finale for the album and is a paean to nature, which again returns us to the theme of the hunter and the hunted. For the animal lovers among us, it's a heartbreakingly powerful song, building from gentler keyboard-led verses to its huge, towering choruses. It's sung from the point of view of various animal species and of the universe itself, from which all known life sprang. The song mourns the fact that our fellow creatures of the world invariably get a hard time from its human inhabitants despite us all being related to them at the deepest level. Most of the verses begin with, 'I dreamed I was...', as Ant imagines being an otter, a red stag, a bear, then a seal. The choruses move back to a universal picture, connecting all life back to 'the sun, the moon and the stars above'. Jeremy Gilbert provides additional keyboards and some delicate harp playing, and the choruses are mightily orchestral in feel. By the final round of choruses, the key shifts upward to add to the drama, finally collapsing via arpeggios and a floating male choral vocal into a two-chord repeating coda, performed on 12-string guitar and Polymoog – the same sequence that closed side one, giving a satisfying feeling of completeness to the album.

I also have a tenuous personal connection with this track as, following the release of my debut album *Earth Magic* in 1989 (which Ant said some kind words about at the time – thanks, Ant!), I toured the album with The Earth Magic Band. We headed for the folk clubs, as I'd become disillusioned with the rock circuit by the late 1980s. During a series of gigs at The Henniker Folk Club in Stratford, London, we noticed the number of floor singers performing songs about hunting, whaling, etc., so we decided to add Ant's song to our set to restore the balance in favour of wildlife – surprisingly, it went down rather well!

Additional Material
'Squirrel' (Phillips)
Poor old 'Squirrel' got squeezed out of the running order of the album at the last moment but provided a B-side for 'We're All As We Lie', the single from the album. 'Squirrel' also turned up on later CD reissues of the album. It's a tender little song in memoriam of a dead squirrel and was written by Ant back in 1970. Featuring just piano and vocals, it's touching in the extreme and delicately performed. Several verses are separated by a piano interlude, which moves from a quiet etude to a more dynamic concerto-like passage, but eventually, we return to the peaceful contemplation of the verses. It's a song that again connects to the theme of the hunter and the hunted – a theme that coloured a series of Ant's songs around this time. This trait was influenced by a boyhood prank with a bow and arrow that sadly ended with the demise of said squirrel. Struck with an immediate and overwhelming sense of guilt, it

proved to be a life-changing moment for Ant in that it solidified a strong anti-hunting bias reflected in a series of his songs on this topic (for example: 'Collections', 'Now What (Are They Doing To My Little Friends)' and dear old 'Squirrel' itself). It's a sad and moving little ode.

'Birdsong Link' (Phillips)
Appearing on the 2015 CD *Private Parts & Extra Pieces*, this lovely interlude was recorded at Essex Studios in October 1977, overdubbed at The Farmyard with the Manor Mobile a month or so later and ex-King Crimson woodwind man Mel Collins added his gorgeous flute contribution at Trident Studios on 13 December 1977. It's a delightful variation on the coda section of the track 'Birdsong', where the fluttering flute and dancing keyboards complement each other beautifully.

'Moonshooter Piano' (Phillips)
The exposed piano track from the recording of the chorus of 'Moonshooter' displays its delicate intricacies. This 56-second snippet was taken from the 16-track master and was recorded at Essex Studios in October 1977. It's another inclusion on the 2015 CD release, *Private Parts & Extra Pieces*.

Private Parts & Pieces (1979)

Personnel:
Anthony Phillips: acoustic and electric guitars, piano, harmonium, vocals
Harry Williamson: 'graphics' ('Tibetan Yak Music')
Recorded at Send Barns, Dorking, Surrey, between 1972 and 1976
Remixed, mitigated and mollified at Trident Studios, London, by Ray Staff
Mastered at Trident Studios, August 1978 by Ray Staff
Remastered at Sterling Sound, NYC, US, by Jack Skinner and Peter Soble
Produced by Anthony Phillips, except 'Tibetan Yak Music', produced by Harry 'pivanaphone' Williamson
Cover artwork: Peter Cross
Record label: Arista (UK); Passport (US)
Released: 23 March 1979, Arista; CD rerelease, Virgin, December 1990; CD rerelease, Blueprint, 1995; CD rerelease, Voiceprint, February 2010 – two-CD set with Private Parts & Pieces II; CD rerelease, Esoteric, September 2015, as part of the box set of Private Parts & Pieces I-IV.

Private Parts & Pieces was the first in an occasional series of releases that started as an outlet for those compositions not finding a home on Ant's more mainstream album releases. As time went by, some of this series became more focused on covering certain styles of composition or those dedicated to a specific instrument. This series provides colourful companion pieces to Ant's main sequence releases, as well as containing some spectacularly good music. This first release neatly mopped up a collection of early tracks and was subtitled 'A Collection Of Guitar And Piano Solos, Duets And Ensembles 1972-1976'.

'Beauty And The Beast' (Phillips)
First up is a composition from 1972, the inspiration stemming from Ant listening to Jeremy Gilbert, who, at the time, was performing a nocturne by Chopin. It employs two pianos, one pin piano (prepared by adjusting pins within the piano) and a classical guitar. A fast-paced, two-note, see-sawing piano motif underpins some extremely speedy and mazy semiquaver runs moving up and down the keyboard and bringing to mind the style of Russian composer Nikolai Rimsky-Korsakov, particularly his short but manic 1899-1900 composition 'Flight Of The Bumblebee'. Some thoughtful panning creates a well-spaced sonic landscape, with an intermittent classical guitar figure panned out to one side, perhaps representing the 'beauty' in the title; the 'beast' may be represented by the ever more frenetic piano runs. These runs almost seem to go out of control towards the end of the piece, buzzing madly across the sound picture as the track slowly fades.

'Field Of Eternity' (Phillips, Rutherford)
This contemplative classical guitar composition, complete with fret squeaks on the chord changes, is a tranquil creation. It was originally part of a longer

piece of the same name that never saw the light of day. It combines themes from a missing movement of one of Ant's larger pieces, 'Flamingo', with an old, then-unreleased Genesis song: 'Pacidy' (since made available on the four-CD box set *Genesis Archive 1967-1975*).

The opening theme elicits a feeling of peace with its slow, stately chord progressions. It falls into triple-time for the descending 'Pacidy' middle section, which is where the Mike Rutherford credit comes in, this part being composed by Ant and Mike in 1969. The finished song was performed by Genesis during a radio broadcast for *BBC Nightride* on 22 February 1970. The 'Pacidy' theme slots seamlessly into 'Field Of Eternity' and nicely breaks the piece up before the opening theme returns to complete one of the loveliest tracks on this album.

'Field Of Eternity' is also the title of Peter Cross's marvellous cover artwork for *Private Parts & Pieces*, picturing what looks like an ever-repeating series of images of the Grim Reaper viewed from the rear. He is wielding a scythe in his hand while reaping a wheatfield, and this image is repeated ad infinitum, running off into the distance along the line of vision. On either side, there are mirror images of an identical rural scene – one side winter and the other side summer. It's an image that's somehow chilling and reassuring at the same time!

'Tibetan Yak Music' (Phillips)

This track was recorded by Ant with the assistance of Harry Williamson, son of noted author Henry Williamson (of *Tarka The Otter* fame). Ant plays a 12-string guitar in a bizarre tuning, while Williamson manipulates a graphic equalizer to treat the 12-string sound. The results have the kind of sharp, spiky sound that aptly reflects the composition's Himalayan title, as some of Ant's 12-string notes emit a crystalline sharpness that mentally transports the listener to the foothills of the Himalayas. It's an interesting sound experiment, placing the emphasis on feel rather than structure. Ant's playing moves towards faster arpeggio picking in the second half of this rumination, over which a more slowly picked guitar emerges over to one side of the stereo picture. After the track fades, it returns for a brief coda. There is a reference on the album cover to the high treble EQ spikes shattering the glass in Ray Staff's fish tank when he mastered the album – whether this is a fact or one of Ant's invented humorous asides is unknown!

'Lullabye – Old Father Time' (Phillips)

Next up is a brief but delicious guitar quartet involving a 12-string acoustic, two six-string acoustics and an electric guitar. It's as peaceful as its title suggests and sports a gorgeous melody. The tune will recur at the end of the album in the shape of the song 'Seven Long Years'. Simple and soothing, it brings to my mind the work of Freddie Phillips and his charming compositions for the series of 1960s BBC TV children's programmes –

Camberwick Green, Trumpton and *Chigley*. On the 2015 CD *Private Parts & Extra Pieces*, there's another 34-second recording of the verse of 'Lullabye-Old Father Time', taped at Send Barns in the summer of 1976, where the guitar quartet is joined by keyboards and a glockenspiel to create a charming mix, reminiscent of the sound of a musical box.

'Harmonium In The Dust (Or Harmonious Stradosphore)' (Phillips)
According to Ant's sleeve notes, this is allegedly adapted from Eustace Grimes' 'Ethiopian Water Diviner's Song' – a tangential reference to Peter Sellers' classic 1959 George Martin-produced comedy album *Songs For Swinging Sellers*, in particular the second section of the third track on side one: 'The Contemporary Scene – 1: Radio Today', subtitled 'The Critics'. This satirical send-up mentions a book by Eustace Grimes called *Harmonium In The Dust* – hence Ant's comment alongside the track's title: 'Apologies to P. Sellers'!
I certainly couldn't better Ant's description of his own recording as featuring his 'dear old lumbering harmonium, set upon by fiercesome (*sic*) Stratocaster'. Possibly the most aggressive moment on the album, the Strat does indeed sound unremittingly ferocious as it besets the swelling chords of Ant's harmonium, but hopefully, the keyboard survived the assault to swell again – an aptly titled piece indeed!

'Tregenna Afternoons' (Phillips)
This 12-string and classical guitar duet closes side one (listed on the LP cover as the 'Home Side'). The piece is a musical reflection, evocative of, in Ant's words, 'languid days overlooking St. Ives Bay from the magical Tregenna Castle in Cornwall'. Anyone who has visited this spot will know how delightful it is, and this music does indeed sum up the relaxed vibe of a summer day on the North Cornish coast. Drifting and ambient in feel, it may be, but it is nonetheless crammed with delightful little themes that build and dissipate like cirrus clouds on a summer's day. After a classical guitar interlude halfway through, some dancing guitar semiquavers summon up the vision of a flock of birds taking off. The piece has a flow akin to the mind wandering on a relaxed, idyllic day in the sunshine. There are some chiming 12-string harmonics at 7.40 as the track winds to its conclusion.

'Reaper' (Phillips)
The so-called 'Away Side' opens with one of Ant's signature tracks of this era, which he refers to as a 'seemingly ageless 12-string solo'. Opening with an impressive combination of chordal harmonics and rhythmic accents, this stirring 12-string composition was composed as part of a planned project for a series of educational releases combining dialogue from Shakespeare plays with music. In 1976, Ant composed this piece, among others, as a potential soundtrack to a performance of *Macbeth* featuring Glenda Jackson and Michael Jayston. 'Reaper' was written as incidental music to accompany a

banquet scene. Unfortunately, the project foundered despite ambitious plans for a six-album set.

Thankfully, much of the music lives on and this track has seen several settings throughout the years: the current glorious 12-string version; a full band version as part of 'The Scottish Suite' on *Private Parts & Pieces II*; a version recorded for Radio Clyde in the summer of 1978 (released on CD in 2003) and a version opening *The Living Room Concert* CD in 1995. 'Reaper' is a richly rewarding piece to listen to and one of Ant's most distinctive and distinguished 12-string compositions.

'Autumnal' (Phillips)

A reflective composition written in 1972, 'Autumnal' was one of Ant's first attempts at orchestration, performed with the Guildhall School of Music Orchestra. It was a piece originally posited for inclusion on *The Geese & The Ghost*. However, the *Private Parts & Pieces* version is quite different, performed entirely by Ant on piano at Send Barns in the spring of 1974. It is an impressionistic study and suits the piano very well, moving from lighter to darker shades as it progresses, contrasting major and minor chords to represent the light and shade of the season that inspired it. There is a persistent rolling feel to its piano arpeggios, but as it builds, it reflects stormier climes with the use of staccato, concerto-like chords but always returns to a more gently reflective contemplation. As it draws to its conclusion, Ant's fingers trip lightly across the treble keys of the piano with some delicate, tinkling arpeggios, bringing the piece to a satisfyingly peaceful denouement. His sleeve notes may illuminate one of the influences on this piece, where he hopes it's not too derivative of 19th-century French composer Claude Debussy.

'Flamingo' (Phillips)

Appreciation of this monster 12-string peregrination will depend upon individual listeners' tolerance of the concerto format, where the whole of the composition is dedicated to one instrument. Generally, my own tastes have a bias towards ensemble performance, where a wider tonal palette generally encourages more colourful sound pictures. In the case of solo adventures such as 'Flamingo', structure inevitably takes precedence over tone colour variation. This piece does follow its own internal logic structurally, though, and for enthusiasts of the 12-string guitar, the track is a dream. Interestingly, despite its 11.06 running time, this is just part of a proposed 12-string concerto! An atmospheric opening of slowly strummed chords gives way to a more staccato theme of scrubbed, rhythmic 12-string. This falls into a third, almost medieval-sounding triple-time, picked theme. These three ideas are constantly played off each other and developed as the piece progresses, along with a very early Genesis-sounding sequence in the style of 'White Mountain' from the *Trespass* album, although a lot more rhythmic than that classic. The overall effect is more rambling than the relatively concise but brilliant 'Reaper' or the exciting, storm-tossed, 12-string adventure that sets pulses racing in the middle section of the title track of *Wise After The Event*, but overall, 'Flamingo' does reward perseverance.

'Seven Long Years' (Phillips)

For me, this is one of Ant's most moving love songs. It reprises the music from 'Lullabye: Old Father Time', but this time, with piano in addition to the guitars. Described by Ant on the sleeve notes as 'a love song for a vanished ballerina', the lyrics again return to the enigmatic Lucy as he turns in one of my favourite vocals of his entire output. It feels almost too personal to listen to as Ant airs his feelings of lost love. His voice starts out singing just the melody, but later, he brings in double-tracked vocal harmonies. There is that wonderful, almost husky cracking feel to his voice that I so love. The tender emotion that radiates from this vocal performance is very moving, as his 'ever hopeless dreaming' for the absent ballerina to return someday closes this lovely song – I guess he must have *really* loved her!

Additional Material
'Stranger' (Phillips, Rutherford)

Appearing as a bonus track on the 2010 Voiceprint CD rerelease of the album, 'Stranger' was penned by Ant and Mike in 1969 and is a typical example of their songwriting style in the interregnum between the two albums: *From Genesis To Revelation* and *Trespass*. This guitar and vocal version, though, was recorded by Ant in October 1990 and proved to be a welcome addition to the Voiceprint reissue of *Private Parts & Pieces I & II*. It possesses a melody that soon finds its way into the subconscious after a few listens. Lyrically, it could well be another song in his 'Lucy' set of compositions, as he sings of 'the star beneath the bright lights' while pondering the strangeness he feels at her absence.

'Silver Song (demo)' (Phillips, Rutherford)

A further demo of 'Silver Song' was recorded by Ant in the spring of 1986 and is included on the 2010 Voiceprint reissue. Oddly, the addition of a new middle eight section, where he reassures his 'baby' that he'll still be here for her, steers it away from its original function as a farewell song to Genesis drummer John Silver and more towards a traditional love song – it's still a fine tune, though.

'Movement IV From Guitar Quintet' (Phillips)

Another bonus track appearing on the *Private Parts & Pieces I & II* 2010 Voiceprint reissue, this is a recording made by Ant in the hot summer of 1976. It is the final movement from a piece also scored for guitar, strings and wind quintet (the first movement of which was performed by Ant on guitar for

Radio Clyde in 1978 and released on CD in 2003. It also featured on *The Living Room Concert* CD in 1995, in both cases entitled 'Conversation Piece').

The attractive triple-time theme that opens 'Movement IV' would indeed sound rather pretty if scored in the ensemble manner suggested earlier. As it progresses, this composition does feel a tad incomplete, though. Around the four-minute mark, it moves to more rapid arpeggio picking for a few minutes before petering out somewhat. It's a piece that, I feel, would surely work better in its suggested ensemble arrangement, with added strings and wind to illuminate its themes.

'Marionette Vignette' (Phillips)

Recorded at Send Barns in the summer of 1976, this short track from the CD *Private Parts & Extra Pieces* is a previously unreleased selection from Ant's very first library music project. It sounds like it may have been intended to accompany a puppet show, as piano and various other keyboards conjure the image of a dancing puppet – it's all very Pinocchio-like in feel.

Sides (1979)

Personnel:
Anthony Phillips: guitars, keyboards, obelisk
The Vicar: lead vocals ('Um & Aargh', 'Lucy Will', 'Holy Deadlock')
Mike Giles: drums
John G. Perry: Wal custom bass
Dale Newman: lead vocals ('Bleak House')
Dan Owen: lead vocals ('Side Door', 'I Want Your Love', 'Souvenir')
Ray Cooper: percussion (tambourine, mark-tree, skulls)
Frank Ricotti: timpani
Morris Pert: congas ('Lucy Will')
Mel Collins: tenor sax ('Side Door')
Ralph Bernascone: lead vocals ('Nightmare' – an instrumental!)
Humbert Ruse: percussion ('Lucy Will'), cor anglais ('Sisters Of Remindum')
Vic Stench: cello ('Lucy Will'), bass ('Bleak House')
Hubert Rinse: dungeon vocals, Moravian yam
Slim Long: C# crampons, tuned bicycle clips
John Hackett: flute ('Souvenir')
Recorded: Essex Studios (October 1978); Matrix Studios (November 1978); Pye Studios (11 January 1979)
Engineer: Richard Austin, aided and abetted by Andy 'Poppadom' Pierce (Essex); Nick Bradford, assisted by Jess 'Herbie' Sutcliffe, Slick Huddersfield, Vic Grimsby and Dick Halifax (Matrix)
Mastered: Trident Studios, Soho, London by Steve 'No bedclothes from Kingsbury' Short, Colin Green and John Brand, helped and humoured by Reno, Craig, Simon, Adam and Simon
Producer: Rupert Hine
Cover artwork: Peter Cross
Record label: Arista (UK); Passport (US)
Released: 23 March 1979, Arista; CD rerelease, Virgin, 1990; CD rerelease, Blueprint, 1995; two-CD rerelease, Voiceprint, April 2010; four-CD definitive edition rerelease, Esoteric, April 2016

Following the release of *Wise After The Event*, Ant was in two minds about which direction to go in for his next main project. Feeling pressured by both his UK and US record companies and feeling that the time possibly wasn't right for his more progressive leanings, he began writing some shorter songs in a more rock/pop style. He managed to keep together the dream team of producer Rupert Hine, bassist John G. Perry and drummer Mike Giles, who had all worked on *Wise After The Event*. Prior to commencing recording, Ant and his assembled musicians rehearsed at The Farmyard in Buckinghamshire for two weeks. This made it a lot simpler once the recording commenced in October 1978 at Essex Studios before moving on to Matrix Studios in November 1978.

Ant's proposed title for the album, *Balls*, was inspired by a comment from one head of A&R who claimed his music 'lacked balls' – which, in turn, inspired Peter Cross, who provided artwork displaying a table soccer game with two teams of Ant-clones: a red team and a blue team facing each other, with a huge collection of balls in the spectator's seating area. If you look carefully at the background, two gaps are visible in the stands, one displaying a miniature of *The Geese & The Ghost* artwork and one displaying elements of the artwork from the cover of *Wise After The Event*. Ironically, the album title was vetoed by both record companies despite Cross's artwork now being complete, so Ant changed the title to *Sides*, which worked rather well in multiple ways. The teams of the soccer game formed sides, the vinyl had two different sides and Ant even managed to split the musical stylings into two different sides: side one displaying his shorter songs and side two highlighting his more expansive, progressive tracks. It all made for a satisfying package in the end.

Sides was released on 23 March 1979 by Arista Records in the UK and on 1 June 1979 by Passport Records in the US. In the UK, the first 5,000 copies of the album came with a free copy of *Private Parts & Pieces*, which hadn't previously been released in the UK. *Sides* was pretty much ignored by the music press at the time, although *Sounds*' Phil Sutcliffe praised its opening track despite dissing the remainder of the album. Most music critics seemed particularly cloth-eared around this era, but thankfully, it's an album that's been reassessed by more switched-on future reviewers and rightly so, as it certainly marked one of Ant's finest main sequence albums and has remained a favourite of mine ever since it first appeared.

'Um & Aargh' (Phillips)

One of the most effective opening salvos on any of Ant's albums, 'Um & Aargh' is also one of his most acerbic songs. It was written in 1978 and inspired by his hassles with record company A&R men through the years. Rhythmic punctuations abound in the intro as Ant's guitar, John Perry's bass and Mike Giles' taut drums hammer out the introductory riffs in tight unison, setting up a tension that remains unresolved in verses built on a repeated six-beat phrase, best seen as a bar of 4/4 followed by a bar of 2/4. On top of this, Ant's urgent vocal crams 16 syllables into each of the six-beat segments, adding to the track's tense, edgy feel.

The astringent lyrics really lay it on the line in their condemnation of the general manner of the jumped-up A&R man in question. It's the closest Ant has ever come to latent aggression in his music, especially so at the end of the first chorus, when he admits he 'felt like shouting something obscene', followed by a growling, hard-to-decipher expletive before the next tense verse resumes! 'Um & Aargh' is undoubtedly one of the best songs on the subject of dealing with record company A&R departments in the 1970s, comparable in its rancour to Queen's damning duo of songs on the same subject – 'Flick Of The Wrist' from *Sheer Heart Attack* (1974) and 'Death On Two Legs' from *A Night At The Opera* (1975). I can fully sympathise with the frustrations expressed by Ant here, as I was similarly doing the rounds of record companies in the late 1970s with the master tape for The Alsatians' debut single and had a comparably bad experience with most A&R men. My eventual solution was the independent route, but Ant would continue to run the gauntlet with these music biz institutions going forward into the 1980s (see the chapter on 1983's *Invisible Men* album).

For me, the tension and release displayed in 'Um & Aargh' give the song its appeal. There is also a catchiness about the cowbell-driven choruses that saw it taken as the single from the album, backed by the non-album track 'Souvenir'. The whole performance of 'Um & Aargh' is topped off by one of Ant's best sustained electric guitar workouts since his solo on Genesis' 'The Knife' from 1970's *Trespass* album. It's a beautifully constructed solo that rises and builds over a bed of guitar arpeggios through expressive chord changes before climaxing in a return to the tense intro riffs. This is followed by one final verse with a few bars added on that compares rock 'n' roll ambition to becoming a 'tin god' destined to eventually plunge into obscurity again. The song then ends on a repeated chorus/bridge on the fade-out.

'I Want Your Love' (Phillips)

Contrasting with the agitated feel of the opening track, this gentle ballad, beautifully sung by Dan Owen, restores a feeling of peace and calm. Over a backing of gently strummed guitar and sensitive bass playing, Owen's vocal imparts deep feeling to Ant's pleading lyrics in one of his most gorgeous love songs. Possibly another ode to Lucy, its lyrics are both poetic and heartfelt. John Perry's bass playing is almost conversational in its tone as he manoeuvres high on the neck of his Wal custom bass with delicate slides and figures that enhance this charming performance. Mike Giles lays back on this number, displaying admirable restraint in his percussive contributions. He brings in a tasteful snare beat, bathed in subtle reverb, for the second verse, but in general, remains unobtrusive. Ant, for his part, adds some deliciously delicate electric guitar decorations; the whole arrangement is a model of economy and an object lesson of how to play in service of the song. Not needing a middle eight to give it balance, the verse and chorus sections alone sound just perfect here. It's one of Ant's finest love songs.

'Lucy Will' (Phillips)

Speaking of the enigmatic Lucy, this next track is totally dedicated to her. It's a catchy and clever song that had me foxed for a while as I attempted to deduce its elusive time signatures. The cascading arpeggio guitar picking of the verses is cyclic and moves around a sequence in 11/8. Despite this quirk, the tumbling vocal melody sung over it has a supreme catchiness. It's astute songwriting, combining an appealing melody with interesting musical invention. Ant reveals a further trick up his sleeve for the chorus, as it's built on a repeating sequence in 15/8.

Along with the cyclic guitar figures, there's an underlying keyboard motif played on one of Ant's synthesisers, which provides a tumbling solo towards the end of the track. The other most notable feature is the contribution of percussionist Morris Pert, who added his congas to the mix during a late session at Pye Studios on Thursday 11 January 1979. The congas add to the commerciality of the track and disguise the fact it has an irregular construction, especially by employing the percussion to cleverly mark the end of each 15-beat phrase during the choruses.

Ant's vocals are passionate and pleading, as you might expect on this subject. The lyrics describe the ballerina Lucy preparing for her performance and then dancing under the bright lights. He also questions whether the renown and fame have lived up to her expectations and whether she still remembers the love they once shared, settling on the optimistic conclusion that, yes, 'Lucy Will' remember.

'Side Door' (Phillips)

Mel Collins makes an appearance on the intro of 'Side Door' as his tenor sax riffs open proceedings, to return later via some linking bridges. With its four-to-the-floor bass drum, rhythmic, choppy guitar chords and funky bass, this track is almost, dare I say it, akin to a dance track. It's certainly the closest Ant ever came to outright funk. It's a catchy song for all that, with a circulatory keyboard motif moving around underneath the choppy guitar.

The vocal is performed by Dan Owen and the lyrics are somewhat oblique, although they do allude to the aforementioned 'Side Door' leading to 'somewhere discreet to let our toupees down', perhaps one of the seedier Soho clubs, judging by the general tone of the light-hearted lyrics! The straightforward dance beat is occasionally interrupted by a bridge consisting of a few bars of tricky time changes – this is Ant we're talking about, after all! The fade-out features some deep vocals on a call and response section in reply to Owen's 'Side Door' chanting, completing this enjoyable diversion.

'Holy Deadlock' (Phillips, Hall)

Opening with some slow, dampened guitar figures, this paean to divorce proceedings creeps along at a gentle crawl. A shaker accompanies the dampened guitar, plucking as we stay on a single chord for the verse. John Perry makes his usual eloquent bass contribution with his subtle slides and runs, and the sing-along choruses feature some swelling synthesiser chords in the background. The track is also decorated with reverb-tinged percussion in an effective but economical arrangement. Although Ant sings the vocals, the lyrics were written by Martin Hall, who has also collaborated with Peter Gabriel as a lyricist. The 'Holy Deadlock' in question is the point at which a marriage breaks down and litigation is involved. It completes the so-called

'First Half' of the album and its varied collection of shorter songs; the 'Second Half', however, will concentrate on the more progressive side of Ant's music.

'Sisters Of Remindum' (Phillips)
The 'Second Half' opens with this magisterial instrumental as Ant plays concerto-like piano chords to announce its arrival. However, this composition is no concerto but a tighter-than-tight ensemble performance that highlights what a brilliant trio the Phillips/Perry/Giles combination is. Over the piano chords runs a delicious and mellifluous synthesiser line that adds to the grandiosity on display here. It also runs with a logic that makes perfect sense musically and these initial variations underline the more progressive nature of the second side of this album. The descending piano figures that stream downwards from the big piano chords are underpinned with some long cor anglais lines, credited to Humbert Ruse (a pseudonym for the hugely talented Rupert Hine – Ant's credits are crammed with in-jokes!). Those long, keening woodwind lines add to the distinction of the opening section.

Then, commencing at 1.40, we fly into an ultra-fast, piano/bass/drums unison section, with Giles' drumming recalling the astonishingly lightning-fast unison runs he played along with on King Crimson's '21st Century Schizoid Man', the opening track from their 1969 debut album, *In The Court Of The Crimson King*. This, though, is less staccato than the King Crimson example but no less astounding in its negotiation of a breathtaking 9/8 time signature. John Perry's bass playing is no less astounding as he traverses this tricky section. It's a dizzying passage that undergoes several modulations before depositing us back with the big piano chords, but this time, supported by thunderous timpani and cymbal splashes. After some trailing piano arpeggios, a more peaceful coda drifts casually into the sunset, floating on piano chords with slow timpani rolls mixed quite far back. It's a singular passage that possibly influenced the similarly drifting piano intro to progressive rock band Big Big Train's later epic 'East Coast Racer' from their 2013 album *English Electric Part Two* (they had previously covered Ant's 'Master Of Time', so they *were* dedicated fans of his output).

'Bleak House' (Phillips)
The next song takes its title from the Charles Dickens novel of the same name, published as a serial in 20 parts during the period 1852/1853. It plays with much of the imagery of the novel rather than attempting to unravel its convoluted plot and subplots. What it does create, with images of black brocade and old iron gates, is an atmosphere akin to an elaborate, historical costume drama. The lyrics are perfectly enhanced by the melodramatic sweep of the musical arrangement, which has the effect of transporting the listener through its many mood changes.

It opens with slow, McCartney-style piano chords a la 'Golden Slumbers', under which a sustained string chord rises and falls, feeling like the sun appearing from behind a cloud before becoming obscured again. To piano accompaniment, decorated by what sounds like a tree-bell, Dale Evans takes the lead vocal as this Dickensian-flavoured tale gently unfolds. In the second half of the first verse, the piano marks time on a crotchet beat as it builds towards the first of the grand, romantic-sounding choruses. These choruses carry a good deal of emotion, as the protagonist, musing on his lover, reiterates: 'She is everything to me', while the romantic sweep of the music is magnified by the string pads that rise and fall in the background. Although still a song, 'Bleak House' sports a more widescreen feel than the songs featured on side one, fitting in perfectly with the more epic feel displayed throughout the second half of the album.

An instrumental middle passage moves to some big chords and huge, sweeping runs on the piano, enhancing the dramatic feel. As the music modulates through a key change, we're eventually deposited back to the gentility of a further verse, where the lyrics paint a scene of a wind-whipped, horse-drawn coach ride along the cobblestone tracks alongside an old canal, perfectly evoked by lightly played but pitching and yawing bass notes fretted high on the neck of the instrument. Although the album credits list Vic Stench as contributing bass to 'Bleak House', the bass passage in question sounds suspiciously like John Perry to my ears. As the dramatization increases, the verse builds, in a similar way to the first one, into a round of the big, emotional choruses, followed by a descent into one last gentle but wintry-sounding half-verse. To close, the piano and string pads that open the song are repeated as the music fades.

'Magdalen' (Phillips)
With its almost madrigal-flavoured opening, this convoluted song, written in 1978, covers a lot of varied musical ground in its 7.39 duration. Ant's guitar parts sound more like a harpsichord in the opening passage. As the lyrics enter, the music takes on a gentle side-to-side sway for its opening verse, falling into a quiet, chant-like section, until at 1.38, the action dramatically changes to a full ensemble performance, introduced by the first salvo of a series of eccentric fills by drummer Mike Giles. As always, his playing forms a hermetic seal with John Perry's tight bass playing. This sets up the pattern of extreme dynamics that characterise the surprising musical variations of this song's arrangement.

Bouncing from full-on ensemble sections to gentler verses, it's a wild ride, although I'm not sure if it's the perfect arrangement for this song – it certainly provides great listening pleasure for progressive rock fans, though. That wonderful rhythm section deserves full praise for the remarkable tightness of the playing, with Mike Giles' series of highly original drum fills being of particular note. He's an incredibly unique percussionist. I was lucky enough to experience Mike Giles' talent in a live setting when, on 26 January 1973, I attended a gig at the Marquee. Giles' one-off band, Q, treated their audience to some delicious playing, as the lineup also included ex-members of jazz-rock band If, as well as Paul Jones (ex-Manfred Mann) on vocals and harmonica. Giles is also one of those individuals with a bizarre sense of humour (for example, check out the album *The Cheerful Insanity Of Giles, Giles & Fripp*, released in 1968). The portentous middle section of 'Magdalen' – commencing at 3.59 – shows the Phillips/Perry/Giles unit at full throttle as they traverse a tricky series of time changes that provide a thrilling slice of progressive rock.

Interestingly, the album credits don't clarify which vocalist is singing 'Magdalen'; it does sound more like one of the other two vocalists rather than Ant, but I'm not certain which it is. Nevertheless, it's a moving performance and the enigmatic and very poetic lyrics evoke the spires and cathedrals mentioned. The song appears to be about an artist painting various landscapes and townscapes, but it also alludes to the Sistine Chapel and Mary Magdalen. Its deeper meaning, though, remains mystifying.

'Nightmare' (Phillips)
The album closes in full progressive rock mode with an instrumental that highlights a further example of this great unit's tight playing. Ant straps on his electric guitar before initiating a series of repeated riffs tied to a bar of seven. This repetitive section is given interest by setting the riff against different chords on the repeats, employing the sequence E minor/B minor/E minor/C major/G# minor/D major as a matrix. It's better described as a repeated 14-beat phrase over two bars of seven. Mike Giles cuts loose on his toms over this riff with typically rolling fills and cymbal splashes, while John Perry marks time with his bass. Some big chords and hammering bass announce a new section, opening with some bobbing electric guitar riffs, joined by a bass pedal effect underpinning them, while building up the pressure is a press snare drum roll from Giles. Ant then fires off some very fast guitar triplets, which speed off at a fair lick. Following this passage, there's an incredible accelerating, then decelerating, guitar/bass/drums unison riff running from 4.07 to 4.14 – it features some truly amazing playing! This riff plunges us back into the 14-beat section that opened the piece, later joined by some big, churchy organ chords with clipped cymbal splashes from Giles.

Compositionally, with its structure built on repeated blocks of sound, glued together by some dynamic unison playing, 'Nightmare' is a somewhat inelegant beast but is redeemed by the galvanising musicianship on display. It does regain some composure via its atmospheric coda, played in the same rhythm but sounding more poignant and less agitated than the main body of the work. It's a fitting capstone to this adventurous and eclectic collection of compositions, marking one of Ant's strongest main sequence albums.

Additional Material
'Souvenir' (Phillips).
This was the B-side to the single 'Um & Aargh' but was restored to the album running order on later CD releases. It's one of Ant's most beautiful and poetic

songs, full of love and longing. Running at 3.45, it may be short and sweet, but he packs a heap of goodness into it. With a bed of guitar arpeggios as a matrix, the vocals of Dan Owen float above. It boasts a gorgeous middle eight that rises from the verses, followed by a brace of subtle musical treats in the shape of some gently serpentine electric guitar noodling from Ant and a stunning, dancing flute solo courtesy of John Hackett. This track is proof of Ant's incredible songwriting ability, a facet sometimes overshadowed by the voluminous amount of instrumental work he has turned out over his long career. 'Souvenir' is a song with perfect form – a real gem.

'Sea Piece Intro' (Phillips)

This interesting 12-string experiment is part of a larger composition that was originally shortlisted for possible inclusion on *Sides* (along with 'Poly Piece' – see chapter on *1984*). Ant's 12-string is panned towards one side of the stereo picture, with strong reverb and subtle treatment of repeat echoes reflecting from the opposite speaker, giving a lovely sense of space to the recording. With my love of this technique, it's a track with huge appeal. Along with Ant's 12-string guitar, at 0.26, there is what sounds like a curious vocalisation that traverses the reverb/echo field, enhancing the unusual atmosphere of this August 1978 Send Barns' recording, featured on the CD *Private Parts & Extra Pieces*, the fifth disc of the Esoteric Records box set *Private Parts & Pieces I-IV* released in 2015.

'Theme From Sea Piece' (Phillips)

Based on Ant's 12-string guitar comes another recording from the 'Sea Piece' set of compositions. Recorded at Send Barns in August 1978, this variation of hypnotic 12-string arpeggios increases its tempo after 42 seconds and the darting 12-string notes resemble fireflies in the falling dusk as notes cascade before our ears, making for an interesting 2.27. This was a further inclusion on the CD *Private Parts & Extra Pieces*.

Private Parts & Pieces II: Back To The Pavilion (1980)

Personnel:
Anthony Phillips: 12-string guitar, classical guitar, electric guitar, piano, vocals, Polymoog, ARP 2600
Andy McCulloch: drums, percussion
Mike Rutherford: bass ('Scottish Suite')
Rob Phillips: oboe ('Von Runkel's Yorker Music')
Mel Collins: flute ('Tremulous')
Recorded: Send Barns, Olympic Studios ('Scottish Suite'), June 1976; Essex Studios, The Farmyard, Trident Studios, November to December 1977; Slick Sound in the North Sea on The Vicar's mobile oil rig ten and sponsored by Ralph Bernascone Aquasports Ltd; put in the right order at Atmosphere Studios by John 'a work of inspired genius' Reiner
Mastered at Trident Studios by celebrated cake maestro Ray Staff
Remastered at Sterling Sound, NYC, US, by Jack Skinner
Producer: Anthony Phillips, Anton Matthews ('Scottish Suite'); Rupert Hine; Anthony Phillips
Record Label: Passport (US)
Released: 28 April 1980, Passport (import only in the UK); CD rerelease, Virgin, 1991; CD rerelease, Blueprint, 1996; CD rerelease with Private Parts & Pieces, Voiceprint, February 2010; CD rerelease, part of Private Parts & Pieces I-IV, Esoteric, September 2015

After *Sides*, Ant's contract with Arista Records in the UK expired, so once he had assembled tracks for a second *Private Parts & Pieces* collection, he relied solely on Passport Records in the US and Canada to secure a release. However, the album proved so popular on import in the UK that it managed to top HMV's import chart. The selection for this second volume of odds and ends proved to be a more eclectic mix than the first *Private Parts & Pieces* collection.

Peter Cross again provided the sleeve artwork, and it was one of his most intricate. There are references to his previous sleeves and a tremendous amount of small detail is visible when scanning the sleeve closely. The small figures, playing cricket on a pitch shaped like the deck of a ship, are representations of the musicians and other personnel involved in the recordings. There is a rather ornate structure at one end of the pitch, possibly representing the pavilion of the album's title. Ant's manager, Tony Smith, dressed in pirate gear, leans from a window; a sailing ship perched on a mountainous wave in the background provides a further nautical reference – if the ship were absent, you could well mistake it for an actual mountain! It's a marvellous cover that is great fun to scour closely for detail. The reverse of the sleeve has many witty photographs of those involved, mostly in cricketing whites, and there are plenty of references to the track titles featured on the album. The credits are also full of humour and mischief, as usual.

Prior to the release of *Back To The Pavilion*, Ant had been recruited by his old writing partner, Mike Rutherford, who had started recording his first solo album at Abba's Polar Studios in Stockholm during a break in Genesis activities. This was the excellent *Smallcreep's Day*, with its side-long title track, based on the Peter Currell Brown novel of the same name. Ant played keyboards on this album, which was released on 15 February 1980 and was Rutherford's only progressive-leaning solo album, as his later releases moved more into the pop mainstream, becoming hugely successful once he formed Mike + the Mechanics.

'Scottish Suite' (Phillips)

Divided into five short movements, this suite covers over 15 minutes of side one and makes for a dynamic start to the album. It was originally intended for use as incidental music to accompany a performance of *Macbeth* featuring Michael Jayston and Glenda Jackson. Initial work on it started at Send Barns in June 1976 with this in mind. The suite was reworked during a five-hour session at Olympic Studios, London, on 19 July 1976 by Ant, along with Mike Rutherford and ex-Greenslade and King Crimson drummer Andy McCulloch. Mixed the next day with the assistance of engineer Anton Matthews, the completed music was subsequently shelved as the Shakespeare project foundered, but thankfully, Ant resurrected the tapes for inclusion on this second *Private Parts & Pieces* release. Retaining the Highland connection to the music's original intention, it became 'Scottish Suite'.

The first movement, 'Salmon Leap', crashes in with big chords, swirling piano triplets and some emotive lead guitar lines from Ant, who is in full electric mode here. Andy McCulloch's drums clatter in after 25 seconds as Ant pulls off some high bends on his guitar and Mike Rutherford's bass drives the fury of this opening salvo. There are several drops into a more becalmed mode, but still with the circulating piano evoking whirlpools and eddies on a Scottish river in full spate. It's easy to imagine the leaping salmon struggling to fight its way upstream, driven by deep instinct, as the music aptly reflects its title. A yearning synthesiser line weaves around above this swirl as the music swells towards a new crescendo. The combination of this rhythm section proves forceful yet agile as they build up to some staccato chords. 'Salmon Leap' is a mighty, tasty slab of progressive rock and makes for a surprisingly muscular opening piece. Some descending piano triplets lead to gentler tinkling on the high notes, and as a drifting synthesiser fades out, our salmon has presumably been successful in his prodigious leap and now resides in the calmer waters above the rapids as his long journey upstream continues.

This new peacefulness is reflected in the second short movement: 'Parting Thistle' (the title is a pun on Scottish football team Partick Thistle). Here, Ant's gentle acoustic guitar performs some touching themes, with a second guitar joining in, recalling the early Genesis acoustic style once again. Mainly a reworking of some of the themes heard earlier on the *Private Parts & Pieces* track 'Reaper', after a few peaceful minutes, the pace again shifts upward for the third section of the 'Scottish Suite'.

This sees the full return of Ant's 12-string classic 'Reaper', but this time in the guise of 'Electric Reaper'. It has the same glorious opening of 12-string chordal harmonics and rhythmic punctuations, but this time with a wonderful electric guitar counterpoint line running around its rhythms. It's a much fuller-sounding reading of the piece than the version on *Private Parts & Pieces* and benefits from some delicious bass flourishes. Around 1.27, some fast, descending guitar spirals lead to a more experimental passage sounding like guitars and bass recorded backwards, achieved by tape reversal.

It's a cleverly arranged section, nodding back to The Beatles' experiments in this area at the time of their 1966 album *Revolver*.

The fourth movement, the amusingly named 'Amorphous, Cadaverous And Nebulous', opens with shimmering synthesiser, combined with some reverb-treated 12-string guitar interjections ranging from strums to fast, twiddly picking. A flutter is applied to the synth line that mimics a sped-up tape sound and is almost comical, sounding akin to a tape unwinding. The fast 12-string picking returns but with a slow, somewhat ghostly-sounding synthesiser line lurking behind it. As the 12-string begins to sound more urgent, the atmosphere slowly builds in intensity until it climaxes with a reprise of some of the opening themes from 'Salmon Leap'. The Phillips/Rutherford/McCulloch combination return for another ensemble performance with clipped, staccato chords and the return of the piano triplets and electric guitar lines that opened the 'Scottish Suite'. It fades on chopped, staccato rhythms, setting up the mesmerising coda of the final section: 'Salmon's Last Sleepwalk'.

This coda returns to the feeling of experiment, with backwards-sounding synthesiser and guitar and more circulating piano – perhaps our salmon has mated but then expired from exhaustion, leaving him dead in the calm, upstream waters? The spectral synth lines drift with the currents, panning from one speaker to another as the coda fades. 'Scottish Suite' is an undoubted triumph and makes a bonnie treat for all of us lads and lassies who love our progressive rock.

'Lindsay' (Phillips)

This reflective piano meditation was recorded at Send Barns in the summer of 1978 and began life with the working title of 'Piano Piece In F'. It's an attractive piece, with Ant's left hand moving evenly across the chords, one note at a time, while his right-hand picks out the melody on the higher notes. There are some subtle modulations as it proceeds, but the piece always returns to the originally stated theme to gently build again. Midway, he plays a lovely figure on the treble notes, very tinkly. The tempo fluctuates organically, magnifying the contemplative feel on display – it's very relaxing music.

'K2' (Phillips)

With the original working title of 'Bonington' (after mountaineer Chris Bonington), this lengthy improvisation on Polymoog and ARP 2600 was recorded live at Send Barns in the spring of 1979. It was retitled 'K2' and named after the second-highest peak in the Himalayas (and on the entire Earth!), a mountain whose summit crests at an elevation of 28,251 feet above sea level.

The music is, as you might expect, ambient in style and the drifting clouds of synthesized sound do indeed conjure a slow and treacherous ascent on the final portion of the gigantic edifice of the title. Quite hypnotic in places, my favourite elements of this performance are the many small piano-like synth figures and deeper bass-end keyboard notes that are treated with reverb and repeat echoes, then panned across the stereo picture. It's a technique I've always loved, whether applied to percussion or musical notes. These interjections certainly enhance the atmosphere of this drifting instrumental. Around the 7.20 mark, the Polymoog waves evoke the irresistible illusion of approaching the mountain's summit, and the track finally peters out at 8.53 as our flag is proudly planted onto the mountain's peak.

'Postlude: End Of The Season' (Phillips)

Providing a brief endpiece to the so-called 'N.O.R. Side' of the vinyl, this short guitar postlude is again in Freddie Phillips territory (no relation, as far as I know!). This was recorded at Send Barns in the summer of 1976, initially for Ant's first batch of library music recordings. He performed a version of it on his Radio Clyde session in July 1978 when it was titled 'Last One To Leave' – a phrase that echoed his earlier song 'Souvenir', which had ended with a plea for 'the last to leave' to turn out the lights. Short on duration but long on charm, 'Postlude' provides the perfect close to side one.

'Heavens' (Phillips)

The 'S.O.R. Side' commences with another of Ant's improvised Polymoog doodles, this time highlighting some descending synth-runs that lead into a churchy-sounding passage. Around 1.20, there are some lovely chords with a big bass-end synth underpinning them. The music becomes quite romantic in places before turning more pensive towards the fade-out. It was recorded at Send Barns in August 1978.

'Spring Meeting' (Phillips)

This is a solo classical guitar rumination recorded in July 1978 at Send Barns. It sports an attractive melody and a strong internal logic in its construction, moving higher on the fretboard as it develops. At 3.52 in duration, it doesn't outstay its welcome and provides a pleasing interlude.

'Romany's Aria' (Phillips)

Next up is one of the refugees from *Wise After The Event* – a link dropped from that album's running order at a late stage. The lineup consists of Ant on guitar and sitar, John G. Perry on bass, Mike Giles on drums and Rupert Hine on percussion. The recording took place at Essex Studios back in October 1977, with overdubs at The Farmyard in November/December 1977. Despite the musicians involved, it gives the impression of a reverse-tape snippet from a larger work.

'Chinaman' (Phillips)

Speaking of refugees from *Wise After The Event*, here's another one! This 'Chinaman', though, is one of a number of references to cricket on the album (including its subtitle, *Back To The Pavilion*), a 'Chinaman' being the name given to a wrist-spin ball delivered by a left-handed bowler in cricket. Musically, this brief track consists of meshed 12-string guitars with some dancing notes on display.

'Nocturne' (Phillips)

This is a classical guitar piece that Ant would revisit on his 2005 album of acoustic pieces, *Field Day*. On its release, he commented that he had risen to the challenge of recording an acoustic album to sharpen up his guitar technique. Evidently, his guitar chops had become rustier over the years due to his more concentrated workload on keyboards, once recording music for sound libraries took up more of his time from the 1990s onwards. It takes a lot of practice to upkeep a technique as prodigious as Ant's! However, back when this original recording was made at Send Barns in July 1978 (at the same session 'Spring Meeting' was laid down), Ant's guitar technique was tip-top. This resulted in a beautifully realised classical guitar meditation with a perfect internal structure. He varies the tone subtly by moving his picking hand closer or further from the bridge, as required. Some effective guitar harmonics are also added later in the piece.

'Magic Garden' (Phillips)

A further track from the *Wise After The Event* sessions, this originally sported the title 'Piano Idea (3 Pianos)' and was laid down at Essex Studios on 27 October 1977 while Ant awaited the arrival of producer Rupert Hine. Richard Austen engineered the session and additional piano parts were overdubbed, adding to its distinctive sound. Slow bass-end piano notes support the more active right-hand melodies as the piece evinces a triple-time lilt.

'Von Runkel's Yorker Music' (Phillips)

This track cropped up on the B-side of the single 'We're All As We Lie' along with 'Squirrel' in 1978. It was also credited on the sleeve of *Wise After The Event* as 'Sitars And Nebulous', although cut from the final running order. The album credits on *Back To The Pavilion* display further examples of Ant's oblique sense of humour and include a mention of 'Neil Von Runkel, the notorious socialist baron who gave up his title and estates to work for the MCC party'. 'Yorker' is a cricketing term for a ball delivered in such a way that it hits the pitch around the batsman's feet.

With Ant on sitar and his brother Rob on oboe, this is basically the chorus tune from 'We're All As We Lie' played on oboe with some sitar strums underpinning it – very pretty! It was recorded at Farmyard Studios with the Manor Mobile during November/December 1977 and produced by Rupert Hine.

'Will O' The Wisp' (Phillips)

Recorded at Send Barns in July 1978, this had the working title of '12-String Flange'. It was improvised by Ant having fun with his 12-string running through an effects unit. Phased 12-string chords, with a large amount of wow and flutter, create a wobbly effect that maybe goes on a bit too long for what it is, clocking in at 3.30. However, the sound does accurately evoke the uncanny natural phenomena of the title – that of phosphorescence dancing above areas of marshy ground, most likely the result of marsh gas combusting and emitting a ghostly apparition that gives this odd natural event its nickname.

'Tremulous' (Phillips)

This title was included in the credits on the sleeve of *Wise After The Event* despite the track being cut from the running order. It may be short, running at 1.06, but it remains a gorgeous little trifle. Ant's fast arpeggio guitar picking was recorded at Essex Studios in October 1977, while Mel Collins added his delightful, coruscating flute contribution at Trident Studios during the final sessions for *Wise After The Event* on 13 December 1977. Although chopped out of the album's running order, this piece is thankfully resurrected here, making a brief but welcome addition to this collection. Ant's guitar fades out at one point, leaving Collins' expressive and reverb-laden flute as he effortlessly weaves his flurries of notes until Ant returns briefly once more – utterly gorgeous!

'I Saw You Today' (Phillips)

His only vocal contribution to the original issue of the album, 'I Saw You Today' is another of Ant's songs of longing, written way back in 1970, just after he quit Genesis. This version was recorded at Send Barns in August 1977. As ever with Ant's vocals, the emotion in his voice is unmistakable as he ponders on a chance sighting of a lost love (Lucy?). With 12-string strums and not much else going on, the vocal is bare, raw and real, especially the 'Oh, how I love you' implorations towards the end of the song, sounding very much 'from the heart'.

'Back To The Pavilion' (Phillips)
The title track is a piano contemplation with a stately melody. It's an early piece, recorded at Send Barns in the winter of 1972, under the working title of 'Passepied' (a title reused for one of Ant's later pieces). It provides a perfect full stop to this collection as it builds through several variations but returns to its main theme, finally closing on a suitable bass-end piano note.

Additional Material
'Lucy: An Illusion' (Phillips)
Prior to Voiceprint Records rereleasing the first two *Private Parts & Pieces* albums on CD, Ant recorded a new version of one of his songs, penned in 1969, whilst he was still with Genesis. The title makes it clear who he's singing about here, and it's a charming song that makes a worthwhile addition to his musical canon. Recorded at Vic's Place in October 1990, it is kept sparse, with just two guitars and vocals. The verses sport a nice chord change, moving from C# to F(sus4) then F, the lilt of which reminds me of the 1911 Charles G. Dawes tune 'Melody In A Major', which, in 1951, gained lyrics by Carl Sigman, becoming the pop standard 'It's All In The Game'. The similarity is not obvious, but that lovely chord change always seems to bring that song to my mind.

Lyrically, it's very much in Ant's poetic style as he acknowledges his illusion that Lucy is with him still, viewing her through 'the panes of my tears'. As with most songs in the 'Lucy' series, it's heartfelt and touching as Ant's emotional vocals illuminate the unfulfilled longing he's feeling.

'Study In D Major' (Phillips)
Recorded at Send Barns in July 1978, this classical guitar piece was published by Josef Weinberger in 1980, along with five other guitar pieces by Ant, under the title *Six Pieces For Guitar*. This previously unreleased recording was included on the 2015 CD release *Private Parts & Extra Pieces*. It is indeed a formal guitar study in the key of D major that proceeds with a geometric logic with strummed chords and line variations as it moves from lower to higher octaves. As it develops, there is a frequent return to the open A-string, giving a drone-like effect to underpin the top-line movements, and some fast, snaking variations are thrown in. Around 4.47, the piece takes on a Spanish flavour before concluding at 5.36.

'K2 Link' (Phillips)
Also included on the *Private Parts & Extra Pieces* CD is this variation on Ant's dedication to the second-highest mountain in the world, K2. Like the first

version, it evokes the rarified air currents moving at over 28,000 feet above sea level via Ant's Polymoog and ARP 2600. Some wavering synth brings us to the summit of this dizzying peak.

1984 (1981)

Personnel:
Anthony Phillips: keyboards, Roland CR78 drum box, guitar, percussion
Richard Scott: percussion, effects, vocal ideas
Morris Pert: timpani, tambourine, gong, congas, bell-tree, vibraslap, marimbas, vibraphone, percussion
Chris and Anita David: vocoder manipulation
Recorded: Send Barns, Dorking, Surrey, August 1980 – January 1981
Completed and mixed at Atmosphere Studios, London, February – March 1981
Produced and engineered by Anthony Phillips, assisted by Richard Scott
Cover artwork: Under The Stairs Productions
Mastered by Ray Staff at Trident Studios, Soho, London
Record label: RCA (UK), Passport (US)
Released: 12 June 1981, RCA; CD rerelease, Virgin, 1991; two-disc CD rerelease, Voiceprint, June 2008; three-disc CD rerelease, Esoteric, June 2016

The release of *Sides* in 1979 brought Ant's contract with Arista Records to a close, and after overseeing the release of his second *Private Parts & Pieces* album in 1980, he turned his attention to his next main sequence project. This time, he decided to tackle a long-form piece that combined the more mechanical rhythms of emerging drum machine technology with classically influenced keyboard sounds. He plumped for a Roland CR78 drum box for the programmed rhythmic elements and turned to his trusty Polymoog and ARP 2600 synthesisers for the keyboard parts. He encountered various challenges during the recording process, not least of which was a fluctuating oscillator in his ARP 2600. In May 1980, two new pieces were realised, dubbed 'Instrumental Single' and 'Strings & Drums', and these eventually became 'Prelude '84' and 'Anthem 1984', used to top and tail the album. The longer title track was split over the two sides of the vinyl album. The final Orwellian title of the album was chosen for its dramatic connotations to move Ant's image away from the dreamier soundscapes he had so far concentrated on. Recording commenced at Send Barns on 14 August 1980 and ran through to January 1981. Ant recorded the album in short segments to be assembled later. He was assisted by his friend Richard Scott, who would be involved in a series of projects with him throughout the early 1980s. The series of recorded segments were finally pieced and edited together by Chris David at Atmosphere Studios, London, in early 1981. Finally, percussionist Morris Pert was booked for a one-day session to add various items of percussion (many of them loaned to Ant by Phil Collins) prior to the mixing of the album at Atmosphere Studios in February and March 1981.

Ant's manager, Tony Smith, managed to secure a deal with RCA Records, along with an advance, and the album was released on 12 June 1981. The cover artwork this time was not by Peter Cross but credited to Under The Stairs Productions and the cover bore the witticism 'Peter Cross is on holiday with Ralph Bernascone' to explain the dark, minimal artwork of the sleeve. Tipping its hat to George Orwell's dystopian novel, it showed a representation of the rat cage from Room 101 against a black background, making for Ant's least attractive album sleeve. Thankfully, Peter Cross would return for many future releases.

1984 did pick up some good notices on its release. J. McAuliffe, in the magazine *Rocking Chair*, called it 'excellent, moody listening', while Joan Tortorici Ruppert, in the *Illinois Entertainer*, reckoned it 'a lean and tidy effort'. Furthermore, Jim Aiken in *Keyboard* magazine praised the orchestration as 'consistently excellent and sometimes spectacular'.

This era also saw the release of another project involving Ant. He had been composing with Harry Williamson back in 1978, and in 1981, some of their co-composed music was employed as the soundtrack to a limited-edition cassette release of a Celtic fairytale by Mother Gong: *The Battle Of The Birds*. Narrated by Gilli Smyth, this recording was again made available in 1987 as a cassette release on Ottersongs with new artwork by Barbara Kirk.

'Prelude '84' (Phillips)

Released as the single from the album, 'Prelude '84' introduces Ant's new sound in a nutshell. In a sideways diversion from his more pastoral output, this album was something of a culture shock for many of Ant's fans at the time. Discovering the joys of the drum machine a year after Genesis had started to employ it on *Duke* in 1980, Ant was keeping up with the changes in musical technology at this point. Musically, the results are mixed but, as ever, interesting. 'Prelude '84' opens with a steadily paced drum box rhythm, ensuring strict timekeeping. Some big, churchy synthesiser chords with a bass pedal effect underpinning them form the matrix for shimmering synth runs up and down the keyboard. A separate, almost jolly theme gives the track its hook and this is doubled with a harmony line on repeat. Some supporting electric guitar lines are audible but low in the mix, as synthesisers dominate. Not for the last time on this album, the musical style of Mike Oldfield is recalled, and RCA did have high hopes for this album, perhaps believing that, sales-wise, it could be a 1980s equivalent to *Tubular Bells*. Sadly, that wasn't to be the case.

The 2016 Esoteric Records three-disc CD rerelease features an early-stage mix of 'Prelude '84', recorded at Send Barns in May 1980, minus later overdubs.

'1984 Part 1' (Phillips)

A throbbing synth intro leads into a stalking, medium-paced beat from the drum box as, under the opening string-synth chords, a bass pedal effect and some bubbling synth noises create an unsettling atmosphere. The synth work reminds me of keyboardist Victor Peraino's distinctive playing on the groundbreaking 1973 synth-rock album *Journey* by Arthur Brown's Kingdom Come. That release was an album that pioneered the use of a drum machine known as the Bentley Rhythm Ace. Ant's Roland CR78 used here was a descendant of this earlier contraption. The advantages and pitfalls of drum machines are neatly summed up by this piece. The reliably steady rhythms programmed into a drum box can be depended on for strict timekeeping, but not so much for creative drum fills – with the best programming skills in the world, it's never going to compete on a creative level with someone like Mike Giles! This becomes obvious in some of the awkward and stiff-sounding drum embellishments heard here, underlining the artificial nature of the genre. The cascading synth arpeggios, however, sound glorious, along with some choral effects. The themes of this composition are cleverly woven, as you would expect from a composer of Ant's ability. As his first stab at a long-form electronic piece, it compares well with a classic of the genre, such as Walter (later Wendy) Carlos' *A Clockwork Orange* (1972), an album that was essential listening for me back in the early 1970s.

About a third of the way through part one, the tempo ups to a speedy pace, with triplet synth arpeggios abounding, before dropping to a more pastoral melody with major and minor shadings that enhance the mood of the piece. The melodies on display are often sumptuous, and a definite Japanese feel emerges from this section. Morris Pert's shaker and various percussion inject a more human element as a new, faster synth section takes hold, adding a sense of urgency to proceedings. The synth lines also become more agitated in a section that underlines the Walter (Wendy) Carlos comparisons. As the synths start to circulate riffs, along with booms from timpani drums, the drama increases. This builds up to a grand-sounding theme where spinning, multi-tracked synth and bass pedal effects abound, until finally, all falls back to a sonar-like synth note that recalls Pink Floyd's 'Echoes' from their 1971 album *Meddle*. The finale of side one rises out of this calmer oasis to weave the earlier themes into a recapitulation with a plaintive, high, piping synth as the big bass end returns to close part one of the album.

The 2016 Esoteric Records three-disc CD rerelease also features an early-stage mix of '1984 Part 1' from the original eight-track master with the drum box absent from the first half of the track (bar some analogue leakage in the background).

'1984 Part 2' (Phillips)
Part two is basically more of the same as the stalking theme that opened the piece returns to stalk again, aided by some Morris Pert percussive interjections that sound startlingly alive against the mechanised plod of the drum box rhythm. The piece benefits from a widely spaced stereo picture, making it easy to pick out Ant's synthesized lines at either side as a crotchet synth rhythm marks time. This is rudely interrupted by loud timpani thumps and a circulating synth line before resuming the slower pace once more. Some effective synth triplets are bolstered by a choral effect in a short break, disrupted by staccato synth blasts. There are some interesting modulations on

Ant's melodic themes, and although remaining sonically in the same ballpark, the piece does display the composer's usual logic in its thematic build.

A police siren effect in one channel plays off against some drum box programming in the opposite channel, accompanied by simulated wind effects, and eventually, it all leads into a somewhat incongruous boogie-like effect from the bottom end of the synth. A sequence of exciting chromatic runs lends the piece a nice touch, and shortly after this section, the music pauses for a short duration. After this quiet moment, shimmering synth chords build back up to the boogie-like rhythm heard earlier and there is a vacillation between these more energised sections and slower passages. Initiating a slow climb to a climax, the instrumental music is split with passages of vocoder and the big timpani breaks return. The vocoder can just be deciphered, quoting the *1984* title of the piece. These contrasting rhythms eventually lead up to an unexpected ending in the shape of one final dissonant synth chord.

'1984 Part 2' also has an early-stage mix featured on disc two of the 2016 Esoteric Records CD rerelease, again minus the overdubbing.

'Anthem 1984' (Phillips)

An ultra-slow drum box rhythm provides the base for some big, spreading synth string chords, reminiscent of The Enid at their most affecting. It's the closest to a romantic feel that this album has achieved. Very much a slow, moody piece to close the album, 'Anthem 1984' was also the B-side to the 'Prelude '84' single, released to promote the album.

'Anthem 1984' also has an earlier mix (without the drum box) on disc two of the 2016 Esoteric Records CD rerelease.

Additional Material
'Ascension' (Phillips)

A study rendered in a sea of floating string-synth chords, 'Ascension' displays a strong internal logic in its slow, magisterial drift. It's easy to imagine this piece scored for a chamber quartet, with its strong classical feel to the fore. Very much in the realm of *Aerie Faerie Nonsense*-era Enid, I'm fond of these floating string creations and have, on occasion, composed and recorded some myself. It all makes for a worthwhile bonus track on the Esoteric Records 2016 three-disc CD rerelease.

'Rule Britannia Suite' (Phillips)

Hereby hangs a tale: in the autumn of 1980, Ant received a commission from writer/broadcaster James Bellini to provide the soundtrack for the six-part ATV series *Rule Britannia*. This programme looked at the upper echelons of the English class system. Ant's brief for this project was defined as 'Vaughan Williams with a twist'. He subsequently laid down some initial tracks at Send Barns in October 1980 before moving on to Atmosphere Studios to record with engineer Chris David, who was a specialist in synchronising music to visuals. Some additional recording was then undertaken at ATV Studios in Elstree over the two days, 25-26 November 1980. The series was broadcast on ITV during July and August 1981.

The 'Rule Britannia Suite' featured on disc two of the 2016 Esoteric Records CD rerelease and was remixed by Jonathan Dann for this release. These mixes are split into six short sections, opening with 'Sally Theme'. This strong theme would find its ideal home on Ant's 1983 album *Invisible Men*, where it would provide the intro/bridge to his fabulous pop song 'Sally', once augmented by Martin Robertson's saxophone figure. Here, it functions more as a kind of overture to the 'Rule Britannia Suite', with a church organ ambience of some grandiosity. The second section represents 'Science & Technology' and does indeed sound more technological, with a pair of oscillating synths playing off each other while bass-synth notes prod at intervals underneath. Part three is titled 'Respect' (obviously *not* a cover of the Aretha Franklin hit!) and is a more regal-sounding synthesized affair, again with some interesting bass-end notes moving under the chords. The fourth section invokes another long-time pillar of the establishment with the title 'Church'. As you might expect, this is mainly a series of big, churchy synth chords that swell majestically. Part five is titled 'Military' and is a slower, measured synth progression, spreading synths out to both channels. The suite comes to an end with 'Power In The Land', which shares a similar synth tone to the earlier sections, including the slowly moving bass-synth note underpin. No surprises there, as the whole thing was recorded by Ant using his Polymoog and ARP 2600 synthesisers. As a suite, it all sounds terribly civilised and was obviously suited to the task in hand of providing the soundtrack to the six-part television series for which it was composed. It's certainly a worthwhile addition to the bonus tracks on the Esoteric Records three-disc set.

'Poly Piece' (Phillips)

Perhaps the most interesting addition to the Esoteric Records rerelease is this long-lost piece recorded at Send Barns as far back as February 1979. Ant intended it for his *Sides* album, but pressure from the record company pushed that album towards a more song-oriented feel. With the title 'Poly Piece', the expectation would be another Polymoog workout, but surprisingly, this is more of an extended piano piece with only low-level synth intrusions.

As a piano piece, it's very much in line with the music that would later be collated by Ant for *Private Parts & Pieces VI: Ivory Moon*, which concentrated on piano compositions only. This is Ant's original demo and is a lengthy beast, running to 16.39. This gives time for plenty of his usual inventive and logical development as the piece progresses. Opening with florid piano arpeggios, it's a hugely organic piece, not tied to one tempo as it speeds up and slows down of its own accord. The piece becomes more fluid as it moves along, with some impressive left-hand work at the lower end of the keyboard to support the occasional excursion towards the highest piano notes with the right hand. There is a definite relationship with the *Sides* instrumental 'Sisters Of Remindum' in its structure and you can see how it would've fitted with the material on the more progressive side two of *Sides* had it been used at the time. As this would've inevitably meant the loss of other material on that album to ensure it fitted with the vinyl format, I think they made the right decision at the time, but thankfully, we now have access to this long-lost piano piece via the 2016 Esoteric Records rerelease. After numerous variations, 'Poly Piece' winds to a close via a perfect classical cadence (chords V-I).

'Long Ago' (Phillips)
Recorded at Send Barns in the autumn of 1980, this short song was recorded by Ant after completing his contribution to the soundtrack of the *Rule Britannia* TV series and just prior to starting *1984*. Accompanied by 12-string guitar, Ant's simple vocal reflects on the loss of a past love, meaning it could be another in the 'Lucy' series of songs, I guess. It consists of a repeated couple of lines with an affecting chorus of 'Who knows?' sung over and over. Despite its simplicity and brevity, it's a lovely little creation and was finally made available after being rediscovered for inclusion on the CD *Private Parts & Extra Pieces*.

Private Parts & Pieces III: Antiques (1982)

Personnel:
Anthony Phillips: classical, 12 and six-string guitars, bass guitar, JD800 string synthesiser ('El Cid')
Enrique Berro Garcia: classical, 12-string and electric guitars
Recorded: Send Barns in June 1981
Mixed by Chris David at Atmosphere Studios, London, August 1981
Mastered at Townhouse Studios, London
Producer: Anthony Phillips
Cover artwork: Peter Cross
Record label: RCA International (UK); Passport (US)
Released: 4 March 1982, RCA International; CD rerelease, Virgin, 1991; CD rerelease, Blueprint, 1996; two-CD rerelease with Private Parts & Pieces IV, Voiceprint, February 2012; CD rerelease as part of Private Parts & Pieces I-IV, Esoteric, September 2016

Ant first met Argentinian guitarist Enrique Berro Garcia whilst mixing *Sides* at Trident Studios in 1979 and the duo finally got to work together in 1981. *Antiques* marked an obvious departure from the previous *Private Parts & Pieces* collections, as it was ostensibly a new project rather than a compilation of older recordings. Most of the compositions here are collaborations between the pair, worked out at casual social gatherings, employing the concept of acoustic, mostly classical guitars, which fitted in snugly with Ant's desire to record an acoustic-based album. There would be some electric guitar contributions, though, added to the project by Enrique Berro Garcia, but the overwhelming vibe of the album remained acoustic. Some older ideas were recycled into a few of the newer compositions, but overall, the material was mostly freshly minted. Sadly, it was to be the last of Ant's albums entirely recorded at Send Barns. The duo set to work there in June 1981, and following recording and overdubbing, Chris David at Atmosphere Studios in London mixed the album in August 1981. As Ant's previous album, *1984,* hadn't done as well as record label RCA expected, they had little interest in a UK release for *Antiques* until Ant's manager, Tony Smith, persuaded them to issue it on their subsidiary label, RCA International, although the nominal advance from them was just one pound! The album appeared in March 1982, just when the Falklands conflict was raising its ugly head. This would cause problems for Enrique Berro Garcia and the enforced repatriation of his family and of Ant's other Argentinian friends at the time deeply affected him, leading to the writing of several penetrating songs about the conflict that would appear on his subsequent album, *Invisible Men.*

At the start of 1982, Ant became involved as a session player with progressive rock band Camel, who had a brief from Gama Records (a subsidiary of Decca) to provide something more commercial for their next album. The band assembled at Abbey Road Studios, London, in January 1982 to record a series of shorter songs and instrumentals for their new album. Ant also contributed to the composing side, co-writing the closing piece on side two, 'End Peace', along with guitarist Andy Latimer, as well as gracing the album with his guitar and keyboard skills. *The Single Factor* was released on 7 May 1982 and was a strong album with excellent playing and a host of memorable tunes. I bought it for the Ant connection at the time, and I still find it enjoyable to listen to. Another session Ant co-produced and played guitar, bass and keyboards on in early 1982 was *Duel*, a solo album by former After The Fire drummer Iva Twydell.

For *Private Parts & Pieces III*, Peter Cross was restored for the sleeve artwork, which is fronted by an antique cabinet displaying artwork miniatures that depict scenes inspired by the music contained within. The reverse of the sleeve shows manager Tony Smith as an auctioneer on a podium that contains the album credits. This is surrounded by various photos of Ant on holiday and of Enrique Berro Garcia.

'Motherforest' (Phillips, Berro Garcia)

This track pretty much lays out the format for much of this third *Private Parts & Pieces* release. 'Motherforest' provides a short but exquisite overture to the varied guitar excursions explored on this album, as Ant, along with his fellow guitarist Enrique Berro Garcia, display an uncanny empathy with each other's playing. Panned to either side of the stereo mix, the duo's classical guitars gently pick out succulent melody and harmony lines. The structure is very classically influenced in its ineffable logic, proceeding slowly but surely, lending the piece a perfect form.

'Hurlingham Suite' (Phillips, Berro Garcia)

Divided into four short movements, this suite is a highlight of side one. The name is possibly a reference to the Hurlingham Club, an Anglo-Argentine sports and social club founded in 1888 by English settlers in Buenos Aires (both Ant and Enrique were keen on tennis and often played together). Its founder, Dr William Cadogan, named it after his home, Hurlingham House, which stands near the River Thames in Fulham, not far from Ant's roots in nearby Putney.

The first movement, 'Ivied Castles', was one of Ant's fragments dating back to 1976. Again, the two guitarists are panned out to either side of the stereo picture, strumming chords with complementary inversions (much like the early Rutherford/Phillips Genesis work). This moves into a slow triple-time rhythm at 1.26 and some chordal picking, evoking a medieval flavour, as it plays off one bass string note. The second part, 'Frosted Windows', started life as the theme for a theatrical play called *What's Inside*, which Ant penned in the summer of 1980. It takes up the previous chordal theme but reiterates it via classical guitars playing single notes in harmony. The wide panning effect means that it's easy to pick out the intricate interplay between them. The piece moves higher up their guitar fretboards as it progresses and is a very distinguished composition, bringing in guitar harmonics. Eventually, Berro Garcia's picked melody is plucked over a shimmering, finger-style chordal backing, which displays a gossamer finesse thanks to Ant's marvellous touch on the guitar. Several alternate versions of this movement were included on later CD reissues.

The third movement, 'Bandido', is possibly the highlight of the piece (it is for me, anyway). Here, Berro Garcia's South American roots shine through as the fast-paced music invokes galloping gauchos on the Pampas with its irresistible locomotion. With a lot more movement on display than the gentler, earlier parts, this is music that's redolent of its title. An almost constant bass string note (mostly an E string, but occasionally modulating to C and beyond) acts as a pedal effect, the return to which gives this piece its taut feel. Several fabulous twin guitar breaks, with mazy runs up and down the fretboard, are a delightful feature of this movement and conjure up a flamenco feel. Some impressive staccato breaks build up the tension as they shuffle up and down like a charmed snake before our imagined gaucho gallops off once more. The final stepped climb of the piece is elating in its ascent, as the two guitars coil and slither upward, with tension-building modulations thrown in, before a brief final descent into a breathless full stop: a perfect ending to this magical 2.46 interlude. The CD reissues featured an additional, slightly slower take of this movement.

After the exhilarating ride of 'Bandido', the final movement, 'Church Bells At Sunset', returns us to tranquillity. Gentle chord work fosters a pastoral ambience, and the final guitar notes imitate the chimes of church bells – a fitting close to this 1.20 postlude.

'Suite In D Minor' (Phillips, Berro Garcia)
This second suite is constructed in three short movements. The first of these, 'Whirlpools', is aptly named, as the fast arpeggios of the two guitars do indeed evoke swirling water. While one guitar continues the sonic whirlpool effect, the other plucks some affecting melodies. When we move to the second part, 'Cobblestones', there's occasional interesting use of dissonance in places. My own favourite part of this suite is the final movement, 'Catacombs'. This is where Berro Garcia adds some surprisingly bluesy electric guitar in the form of an impressive solo, to which Ant replies with some nifty acoustic playing, making a wonderful close to the suite and side one of the original LP. Later CD reissues added an alternate version of this track.

'Danse Nude' (Phillips, Berro Garcia)
Side two opens with a purely experimental offering in the form of guitars recorded backwards by tape reversal. It's a carefully worked piece and very enjoyable. The title is a partial anagram of a track further on into side two, 'Sand Dunes', and this is because a theme running in 7/8 time from this latter

recording has been recorded in reverse here. The backward guitars exude the characteristic 'sucking' sound caused by this technique. This is especially effective in the ending, where the track vanishes in a halo of reverb – I love it!

'Esperanza' (Phillips, Berro Garcia)

Ant's 12-string guitar picking on 'Esperanza' is close to the sound of a harpsichord and makes a perfect matrix for Berro Garcia's electric guitar lines with their overlapping melodies; he even throws in some harmony guitar lines a la Wishbone Ash. It's another intricately worked-out piece and the CD reissues include an additional mix that highlights Ant's 12-string guitar, minus Berro Garcia's melody lines.

'Elegy' (Phillips, Berro Garcia)

With slow chordal acoustic guitar strums in one channel and a classical guitar in the other, 'Elegy' is a fetching slow interlude with some nice chord shifts. The initial idea slowly modulates through some ear-pleasing changes, developing the original sequence.

'Otto's Face' (Phillips, Berro Garcia)

The bouncing acoustic guitar plucking that opens this track sounds almost pizzicato, giving the effect of water droplets rebounding from the ground. Moving organically, this opening increases its tempo before slowing again as a second guitar plays cascades of notes. Eventually, the piece moves to a slower tempo with lots of tasty interplay between the two guitarists as it moves from lighter to darker shades via major and minor chords. Towards the end, it settles on a bass string riff that is almost 'rock 'n' roll' in its feel. It's a track with lots of subtle dynamics.

'Sand Dunes' (Phillips, Berro Garcia)

As mentioned earlier, part of this track was reversed for 'Danse Nude' – the side two opener. 'Sand Dunes' is quite a long, contemplative track with developments built on two different themes. The first of these is in slow triple-time and opens the piece with rest bars after every phrase, perhaps reflecting the slowly building and dissipating sand dunes of the title. The theme firms up to a more complete swaying rhythm as it's developed. At 2.16, an interesting new theme enters, built on a 7/8 time signature, and this, too, moves through variations as it proceeds. Moving between this new theme and the original one, the track is quite successful in evoking the shifting vista of a desert landscape and certainly justifies its 8.24 running time.

'Old Wives Tale' (Phillips)

Closing side two is this pretty tune written by Ant way back in 1968 when it was a song called 'Little Leaf' and was part of the Genesis live set during their earliest gigs. Encapsulating the wondrous naivety abroad in the late 1960s era, when the future looked hopeful and exciting and anything seemed possible, it sums up what I love about very early Genesis, and despite being reworked by Ant in June 1981, its triple-time arpeggio picking and charming melody still retain the unique flavour of the age in which it was written.

Additional Material

'El Cid' (Phillips, Berro Garcia)

Although this technically falls outside the remit of this book, recorded at Vic's Place in the summer of 1994, the fact that it was included on later reissues of *Antiques* means that I will give it a brief mention here. It sounds like a guitar improvisation played over some atmospheric string chords from Ant's JD800 string synthesiser. With a strong Moorish flavour, crossed with flamenco influence, the classical guitar wanders wide and free over Arabic scales, reflecting the filmic title of the piece. It makes a fine addition to the album.

Invisible Men (1983)

Personnel:

Anthony Phillips: vocals, Colorama electric guitar, Yari classical guitar, Ovation bass guitar, Polymoog, Jupiter 8 synthesiser, ARP 2600 synthesiser, Rickenbacker 12-string guitar, Mellotron, Fender Stratocaster electric guitar, Hammond organ L-100, acoustic 12-string guitar, tubular bells, piano, Les Paul electric guitar, Fender Rhodes electric piano

Richard Scott: vocals, Roland 808 drum machine, vocoder, Fender Stratocaster electric guitar

Joji Hirota: marimbas, wood blocks, tambourine, shaker, jawbone, cabasa, bell-tree, timpani, darabukka, cymbals, cowbell

Paul Robinson: drums ('The Women Were Watching', 'Going For Broke')

Jonathan Snowdon: piccolo

The Vicar: church organ

Jeff Dunne: drums

Martin Drover: trumpet ('Love In A Hot Air Balloon', 'It's Not Easy'), flugelhorn ('Falling For Love')

Uti Koofreh: backing vocals ('Going For Broke', 'It's Not Easy')

Martin Robertson: soprano saxophone ('Sally', 'Golden Bodies')

Morris Pert: tambourine, shakers, jawbone, cabasa

Bimbo Acock: saxes, flute, brass arrangements

Malcolm Griffiths: trombone ('It's Not Easy')

Henry & The Cakettes: party ('Love In A Hot Air Balloon')

Ralph Bernascone: sarrusaphone ('Guru')

Vic Stench: bass, contrabass, camp bass ('I Want Your Heart')

Recorded: Englewood Studios, April – September 1982, Atmosphere Studios, October – December 1982

Produced and engineered by Trevor Vallis, Anthony Phillips and Richard Scott

Record label: Passport (US), Street Tunes (UK)

Released: 24 October 1983, Passport (US); 13 April 1984, Street Tunes (UK); CD rerelease, Virgin, 1991; CD rerelease, Blueprint, 1995; two-CD rerelease, Esoteric, October 2013

After Ant relocated to South London in the early 1980s, he needed a boost to his income to shore up a flagging financial situation, hence his contemplation on recording something of a more commercial bent. His long-time US record company, Passport, encouraged him in this direction, so after completing recording for *Private Parts & Pieces III*, he began gathering material together with a view to a song-oriented album. He had recently been writing some songs with his friend Richard Scott for a potential musical based on the Kit Williams book *Masquerade*. Although this musical never saw the light of day, much of the music from it would slowly emerge over time via his *Private Parts & Pieces* series. Already armed with a trio of songs written the year before, Ant set to work with Richard Scott to demo songs for his next project.

Above: Anthony Phillips looking the very essence of the eccentric Englishman at peace with his pipe in the 1970s.

Left: Seven years in the making, Ant's 1977 debut album, *The Geese & The Ghost*, proved to be well worth the wait. (*Passport Records*)

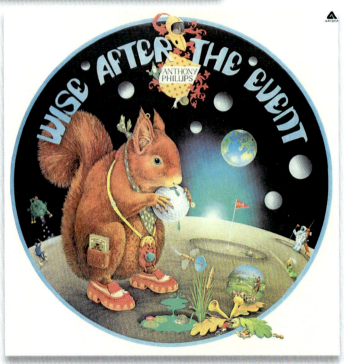

Right: With its whimsical songs and top-notch musicianship, *Wise After The Event* displayed Ant's wilful musical eclecticism. (*Passport Records*)

Right: The first in Ant's occasional series, highlighting previously unreleased recordings, *Private Parts & Pieces* proved a welcome adjunct to his main sequence releases. (*Passport Records*)

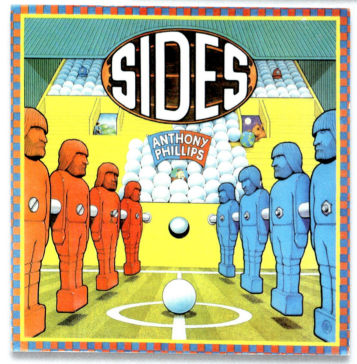

Left: Supported by the superb musicians from *Wise After The Event*, *Sides* displayed Ant's songwriting and his more progressive tendencies. (*Passport Records*)

Above: Ant looking every inch the ex-public schoolboy, with his college scarf flying behind him, in the early 1980s.

Above: A Dutch advertisement promoting the release of Ant's debut album, *The Geese & The Ghost*, in 1977.
Below: Ant's ex-Anon and Genesis bandmate and musical collaborator Mike Rutherford playing his Rickenbacker 12-string/bass, double-neck guitar. (*Getty*)

Above: Ant in the 1980s, looking as if his new studio is under construction in the background!
Below: The multi-talented musician Rupert Hine at the studio controls; he produced both *Wise After The Event* and *Sides* for Ant. (*Getty*)

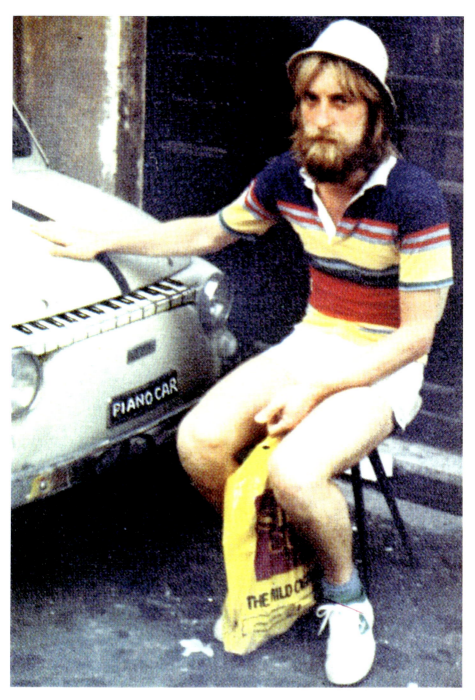

Above: A rather downbeat-looking Ant on holiday – this photo featured on the back cover of *Private Parts & Pieces III: Antiques* in 1982. (*Passport Records*)

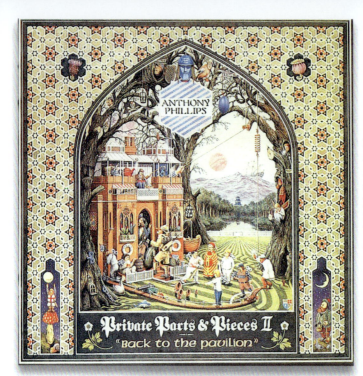

Left: The second *Private Parts & Pieces* volume, released in 1980, proved to be even more varied than the first. (*Passport Records*)

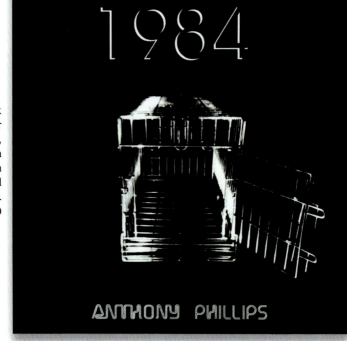

Right: A shock to the system for many Ant followers, *1984* found him exploring drum machines and modern technology. (*Esoteric Records*)

Right: Recorded with Argentine guitarist Enrique Berro Garcia, *Antiques* was the first *Private Parts & Pieces* volume to be a complete project. (*Passport Records*)

Left: *Invisible Men*, recorded with Richard Scott and released in 1983 in the US, saw Ant moving towards pop songwriting. (*Esoteric Records*)

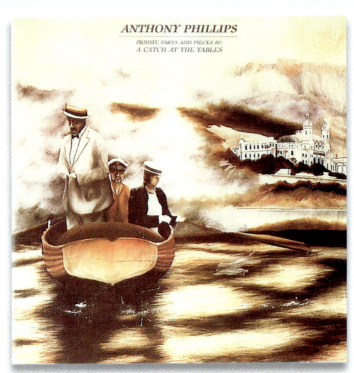

Left: *A Catch At The Tables*, the fourth *Private Parts & Pieces* volume, contrasted guitar pieces with synthesizer improvisations. It also featured the superb song 'Sistine'. (*Passport Records*)

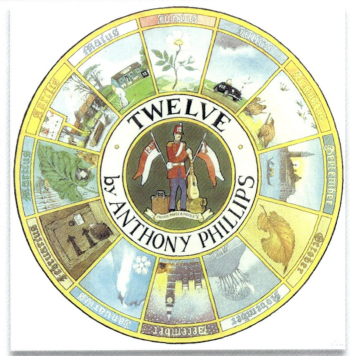

Right: A complete album of 12-string guitar pieces made up *Twelve*, the fifth volume of *Private Parts & Pieces*, released in 1985. (*Passport Records*)

Right: Ant cradling his beloved 12-string guitar on the rear sleeve of *Private Parts & Pieces V: Twelve*. (*Passport Records*)

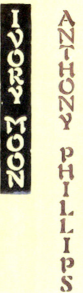

Left: *Ivory Moon*, the sixth volume in the *Private Parts & Pieces* series, highlighted Ant's piano compositions from 1971 to 1986. (*Passport Records*)

Left: Ant in the garden with his beloved Fender Stratocaster of many years vintage. (*Getty*)

Right: Ant's collaboration with Mother Gong, *Battle Of The Birds*, was another limited-edition cassette release in the 1980s. (*Ottersongs/Barbara Kirk*)

Left: A 1983 publicity shot for the newly christened Anthony Phillips Band, L-R: Joji Hirota, Ant and Richard Scott.

Right: The limited-edition cassette *Tarka Music* saw the release of the original *Tarka* demos in 1987. (*Ottersongs/ Barbara Kirk*)

Left: Ex-King Crimson drummer Mike Giles gave something special to both *Wise After The Event* and *Sides* via his percussive contributions.

Right: Virtuoso percussionist Morris Pert added a welcome human element to Ant's technologically based *1984* album.

Left: With its bias towards synth improvisations, *Slow Waves, Soft Stars* found Ant penetrating the burgeoning New Age market in 1987. (*Audion Records*)

Right: Thirteen years in the planning, Ant's orchestral suite *Tarka,* composed in collaboration with Harry Williamson, was finally released in 1988. (*PRT Records*)

Right: *Finger Painting*, Ant's first compilation of library, film and TV music, was released on a limited-edition cassette in 1989. (*Occasional Records*)

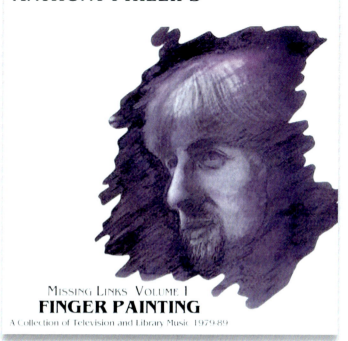

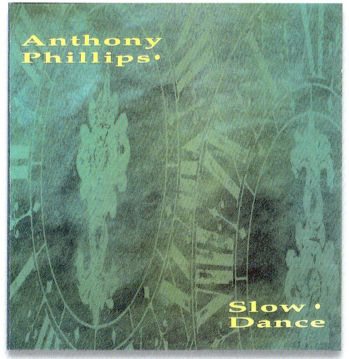

Left: *Slow Dance*, released in 1990, proved to be the culmination of Ant's long-form composing ambitions. (*Virgin Records*)

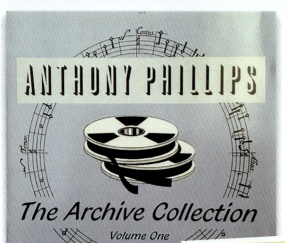

Left: Released in 1998, *Archive Collection Volume I* featured many unreleased recordings from Ant's pre-1990 period. (*Blueprint Records*)

Right: *Archive Collection Volume II*, first released in 2004, neatly gathered up another interesting batch of Ant's archive material. (*Blueprint Records*)

Left: Music from Ant's long-lost *Masquerade* project appeared as a bonus disc on the CD box set *Archive Collection Volume I And Volume II* in 2022. (*Esoteric Records*)

In April 1982, recording commenced at Englewood Studios, which was, in fact, Ant's new home studio in Clapham, South London. The duo initially made speedy progress, committing the basis of 28 new songs to tape in strict daytime sessions. Some of these recordings would be held back and a selection would appear on *Private Parts & Pieces IV* in 1984. As *Invisible Men* was planned as a song-oriented vocal album, Ant took singing lessons from experienced musician and conductor John Owen Edwards, who had also tutored Mike Rutherford. The vocals would end up being shared between Richard Scott and Ant, as they were the songwriting team for this more pop-inclined project.

By October 1982, it was decided to take advantage of the 24-track facilities at Atmosphere Studios in West London and 18 of Ant's eight-track masters were selected to work on during this second phase of recording, concentrating on vocals and overdubs. It was at this stage that Ant began to have doubts over the integrity of the project and was growing weary of listening to some of the poppier selections to the extent that in an interview in issue 31 of *Genesis Magazine*, dated April 1984, he claimed: 'some of the poppy ones were just palling so badly – from palling to appalling.' This was six months into the project and the initial speedy recording schedule had, by now, slowed to a crawl. The duo had also roped in recording engineer Trevor Vallis to oversee the production. Several drummers were brought in to augment the initial drum box percussive tracks in the hope of beefing up the drum sound. As Ant later acknowledged, what they really needed was a producer of the calibre of Rupert Hine and a rhythm section with the chops and the clout of John G. Perry and Mike Giles!

The first master of the completed album was cut in New York for US release on Passport Records, although Ant also received complaints from the cutting engineers over there, who moaned subjectively about the sound of certain tracks, suggesting a remix. Once it became clear that this would increase the budget, they finally decided to go with what they already had. The album first saw the light of day as a US-only release on Passport Records on 24 October 1983 and was only available on import in the UK that year. I remember eagerly acquiring my import copy at the tail end of 1983 and being impressed by Ant's songwriting skills and the clever pop production touches despite the composer's own doubts about the project.

A new deal was negotiated for the album's UK release with a smaller independent label named Street Tunes. The UK version differed from the US release in that the track 'Exocet' was replaced with 'It's Not Easy' and the running order was changed, the album now opening with 'Golden Bodies' rather than 'Sally'. The latter of these two songs was released as a 12" single, along with two Falklands War-influenced tracks: 'The Women Were Watching' and 'Exocet'.

The UK album artwork for the original vinyl release consists of two poorly drawn figures filled in with random typeface, like jumbled newsprint. If you look carefully at the blue and yellow colours within the figures, it's possible to discern cut-up photos of the duo's faces peering out. The cover has 'The Anthony Phillips Band' printed at the top and on the rear of the sleeve. On the US version, a small red sticker attached to the shrink wrap packaging was used at the time to proclaim, 'The New Anthony Phillips Band!', and the cover of the original vinyl US release employs one of the publicity shots taken by photographer Stephen Marsh to promote the album. The chosen photo – of Ant standing and Richard Scott seated – has been modified so that Phillips and Scott look like anonymous figures, with their facial features faded out (apart from their hair and Ant's beard!), set against coloured blocks of pink, blue, green and yellow. This image is employed on the reverse of the UK version. The album credits bear the legend: 'Peter Cross was left on holiday by Ralph Bernascone', indicating that this design was not the work of Ant's usual, excellent cover artist!

As the rereleases jiggled the album's running order around, it was difficult for me to decide what order to present the tracks in here, but I've decided to go with the US release simply because that was the only version available when the album first appeared in October 1983. The UK release didn't emerge until Friday 13 April 1984.

'Sally' (Phillips)

This song was developed from a piece used as incidental music for the 1981 ATV television series *Rule Britannia* (see chapter on *1984*). 'Sally' was released as the single from the album in the then fashionable 12" format. The song makes for a fine start to the album, as Martin Robertson's blowsy soprano saxophone grabs the attention on the intro, much like Raf Ravenscroft had done with his indelible sax figure on Gerry Rafferty's 'Baker Street' five years earlier. Richard Scott's Roland 808 drum box drives the rhythm, enhanced by percussionist Joji Hirota's marimbas and wood blocks. At the time, Hirota featured in many of the publicity shots taken to promote the (somewhat bogus) band image encouraged by record company management, which created the illusion of a three-piece Anthony Phillips Band. Very much my own favourite song from this album, 'Sally' is driven by Ant on various keyboards and his Fender Stratocaster, as well as bass. The writing was completed by Ant in 1981. It has an irresistible pop drive and forward locomotion as it charges through a repeated verse/bridge/chorus structure, with several returns to the galvanizing soprano saxophone figures that opened it.

Lyrically, it displays Ant's usual elan for words as we follow Balham Johnny's attempts to pursue a socially unobtainable PR queen named Sally in an engrossing lyric which warns cloudy-eyed Johnny, 'She's spinning you like a circus wheel'. Mind you, he can't seem to leave her alone and sounds like something of a stalker himself! The chorus is extremely catchy, and with more airplay, there's a definite feeling that this could have been a hit single contender had more people heard it at the time. It's a fine example of Ant's skill at pop songwriting.

'Golden Bodies' (Phillips, Scott)

Opening with the Roland 808 click-clacking away, along with a shout from somebody, we're soon into a sub-tropical sounding vibe as Martin Robertson's soprano saxophone returns to the fray, this time playing a sensuous melody that makes a great opening hook. Ant again takes the vocals on a song of longing for a life of surf, sand and tanned bodies on some faraway beach while he's daydreaming 'on the seventh floor' of an apartment block. He plays his Colorama electric guitar, as well as a variety of synthesisers. The hooky choruses are driven by an elastic-sounding bass guitar. The Caribbean flavour of the song is also greatly enhanced by the marimba playing of Joji Hirota.

Originally, this song was intended for singer Sheena Easton, but due to a change of management, it ended up being covered by Little Foxes, a three-piece female vocal group. This cover version was released as a single on the C&D imprint in July 1983, three months prior to Ant's version on *Invisible Men*.

Disc two of the 2013 Esoteric CD reissue of the album includes a demo of this song with a different set of lyrics to the studio version.

'Going For Broke' (Phillips, Scott)

Richard Scott takes the vocal honours on this song of unabashed optimism, where the protagonist is determined to 'shoot the moon' and indeed go for broke. The big, dramatic intro is all crashing timpani, courtesy of Joji Hirota, while the addition of real drums, played by Paul Robinson, gives the track some serious bottle. It also boasts lots of Ant's incisive electric guitar as he wields his Strat with intent and cuts loose on some impressive soloing throughout. As well as the Strat soloing, he also employs his Rickenbacker 12-string guitar, although, in the bluster of the intro/bridge sections and the frantic, motoring verses, this doesn't make as much of an impression as his fluid lead lines do. All in all, 'Going For Broke' makes for a satisfying, up-tempo pop/rock interlude.

'Exocet' (Phillips, Scott)

Things get a bit more experimental with this track, the first of a pair of songs on *Invisible Men* influenced by the Falklands conflict. Both Ant and lyricist Richard Scott were deeply affected by the awfulness of what was, initially, at least, a preventable war. Argentinian sabre-rattling over the Malvinas was obvious a year or so prior to the conflict, but unfortunately, no action was taken to deter an invasion by shoring up the defences of the Islands at that time.

The song takes its title from the French-built anti-ship missile that caused such devastation during the conflict. 'Exocet' creeps forward on a slow but steady subaquatic throb as the music pulses with a feeling of approaching menace. Ant's subsonic Mellotron chords intensify the atmosphere, along with the oscillating thrum of his Polymoog and ARP synthesisers. His lead vocals are backed with an aquatic choir, along with what is credited as 'lift shaft vocals'. It's certainly a track that strongly evokes its subject with an overwhelmingly claustrophobic feel, exacerbated by a constant synthesized throb as the Roland 808 drum box clatters relentlessly forward. The killer punch arrives with drummer Jeff Dunne's tumbling, gated tom-tom fills, which add a sense of impending doom, as well as recalling the then-recent, game-changing percussive experiments of the album *Peter Gabriel 3* and the early 1980s Genesis and Phil Collins albums. There are also various random synth figures treated with repeat echo that bounces around the sound picture like sonar reflections, adding to the atmosphere of unease.

The lyrics cleverly build on this intense atmosphere with an evocation of ocean waves, rain and the inevitability of certain death. The track ends chillingly on a lone Mellotron chord, cutting into a sample of MoD spokesman Ian McDonald delivering a matter-of-fact statement to the press about the 200-mile exclusion zone imposed around the Falkland Islands by the UK government in April 1982.

'Love In A Hot Air Balloon' (Phillips, Scott)

Happily, it's back to whimsical humour on this appealing, upbeat pop tune expounding the joys of hot air ballooning. The bouncy beat is buoyed by some mid-period Beatles trumpet figures, a la 'Penny Lane', played by brass man Martin Drover. These link the springy, joyous verses and choruses in which Ant celebrates the local Surrey/Sussex landscape he'd spent much of his life in, as viewed from the vantage point of a drifting hot-air balloon. The line that always makes me smile is his observation of the aerial advantage of 'no bottlenecks on the A23'. The 'me-oh-my' choruses are catchy in the extreme, and the whole track exudes a highly infectious sing-along vibe. Richard Scott utilises Ant's Strat for some guitar interjections, while Joji Hirota's varied percussive contributions smooth the track's forward motion, along with Jeff Dunne's drums. Halfway through, various studio guests represent a kind of aerial party in progress with their whoops, hollers and laughter, credited on the sleeve to Henry and the Cakettes. It's all good fun, adding to the intriguing balance of styles and moods displayed on this album.

'Traces' (Phillips, Scott)

This steadily paced love song is a duo performance, with Richard Scott on Roland 808 drum box and vocoder, while Ant provides vocals, guitars and keyboards. A song of lovelorn yearning, it provides a more poignant interlude to close side one. Ant generates some real emotion in the vocal department, especially in the choruses, even though the lyrics were penned by Richard Scott. There are some nice downward swooping guitar glissandi on the verses that add to its swooning melody.

'I Want Your Heart' (Phillips, Scott)

Side two of the US edition opens with this interestingly constructed upbeat pop song. The straight 4/4 verses lead into choruses that move into fast 7/8 time, giving a quirky feel to this drum box-driven track. These choruses sport the catchy title refrain despite employing an odd time signature. It's an all-action track with lots of movement, complete with a well-constructed, repeated middle section displaying some nice chord changes. The three distinct parts of the song are linked by an effective bridge, built on the chorus chords, as Ant brings some tubular bells into action among the frantic synth lines. Richard Scott sings this paean to a rebounding love affair. It's a song with a persistent pop drive and boundless energy.

'Falling For Love' (Phillips, Scott)

Fading in on a measured Jeff Dunne drum intro, another Richard Scott vocal graces this delicious pop ballad. Ant goes mellow on his Fender Rhodes electric piano, along with some seductive, sliding bass guitar, which suits the song perfectly. There are charming backing vocals in the choruses, performed by the duo as Jeff Dunne's laid-back drums are bolstered by Joji Hirota's shaker contribution. Midway through, Ant provides a tasteful, understated guitar solo on his Strat before Martin Drover returns for a light, feathery flugelhorn solo of absolute perfection – a real highlight of this track. Ant revisited this song in the spring of 1986, and this country-tinged alternate version, which was recorded at Vic's Place, is included on disc two of the 2013 Esoteric CD reissue of the album.

'Guru' (Phillips)

'Guru' opens with parping, punctuating brass stabs, arranged by Bimbo Acock, as Ant serves up some tasty electric guitar bends as backup to a section that also functions as a bridge later in the song. The laid-back groove drifts seductively and Bimbo Acock's saxes and Martin Drover's trumpet are prominent in an understated but clever arrangement. Ant employs four different guitars on this track – his Strat, Les Paul, Colorama and 12-string – as well as some shimmering Polymoog, organ, Fender Rhodes electric piano and bass. Richard Scott's Roland 808 drum box provides the rhythmic foundation, while percussionist Morris Pert backs this up with shakers, jawbone and cabasa.

The song deals with the potential dangers of religious brainwashing as the protagonist declares his love and concern for a female partner who has evidently been inducted into a certain red-robed religious cult, making the continuation of their relationship rather difficult. The male partner has no need for a guru and expounds upon his fears for her, proclaiming: 'They're taking your name away'. Written by Ant in 1981, it was one of the three original numbers first earmarked for *Invisible Men*. It's a gorgeous-sounding track on a serious and sombre subject.

'The Women Were Watching' (Phillips, Scott)

The second song written in response to the Falklands' conflict, this upbeat but tense-sounding track stomps solidly along on Paul Robinson's drumbeat, with Ant's Colorama electric and Rickenbacker 12-string guitars treated with a flanging effect as he picks to-and-fro across the verse chords. Jonathan Snowdon's piccolo interjections are the masterstroke here, as he plays short excerpts from 'The Sailor's Hornpipe' every few bars, amplifying the nautical flavour of the lyrics. The first verse portrays the jingoism of the cheering, flag-waving crowds at Portsmouth Harbour as the ships of the task force leave, bound for the South Atlantic. It mentions sailors' wives with 'anxious eyes' – the women who were watching along the shore as their men went off to war. The choruses are buoyed by crash chords from Ant's guitar, and the whole track retains a tangible tension that never lets up despite the up-tempo beat, which befits this subject. The second verse focuses on one couple during the night before that sailor's departure. It brings home the realities of war and the trepidation felt by the families involved.

'My Time Has Come' (Phillips)

If any track underlines what a fine songwriter Ant could be on an inspired day, it's the closing track of the album: the deeply mysterious and spellbinding 'My Time Has Come'. Along with 'Exocet', it's the track that leans the most towards experimentalism via its striking sound collage section. The beguiling chord sequence fosters a sense of mystery, and once combined with the poetic sweep of Ant's enigmatic lyrics, it weaves a subtle magic. Using portentous imagery, it's more aligned in feel to some of the material on *Wise After The Event*. The verses are driven by Ant's 12-string guitar as he gently strums and sings, but the choruses, although still at the same slow tempo, are more dramatic, lifted by Joji Hirota's booming timpani drums and cymbals. There is clever employment of Ant's synthesisers and Mellotron throughout, adding to the slowly creeping atmosphere as we meet various perplexing characters, including Father Eli and his rocking chair; the secret dreamer, Yena; a pair of Baronesses playing a hand of whist and, inevitably, the Monolithic Host. It reads like some epic poem from mythology, and although superficially impenetrable, the lyrics do lean towards symbolism, just begging to be interpreted.

I experienced my own chilling moment while listening to this track not long after the Lockerbie air disaster in December 1988, where a Pan Am airliner was targeted with a terrorist bomb, incurring an appalling loss of life. The third verse of 'My Time Has Come' appears to describe a similar catastrophe and the couplet, 'They're all out on Pan Am 109/The giant's melted into thin air', sent a chill up my spine, sending me scrambling to check the number of the flight that had disintegrated over Lockerbie, thinking Ant had come up with a future-predicting 'Nostradamus moment' six years prior to the event (it turned out to be Pan Am 103, not 109). To this day, it's still a verse that gives me chills when I listen to it!

A close inspection of the lyrics in the final verse perhaps hints that Ant was maybe couching this puzzling tale in terms of relativity, as evidenced by the line, 'I might not get back till you're old', putting the song in a similar territory to Brian May's lyric for his song "39' (from the 1975 Queen album *A Night At The Opera*), which deals with a similar relativistic concept. Whatever, it's an unusual topic to pick for a song and 'My Time Has Come' retains its sense of ambiguity.

One of the most interesting moments in this remarkable recording is the sound collage that occurs after the second chorus. This collection of abstract sounds was achieved by combining traffic noise outside the studio, recorded by Richard Scott on his Sony Walkman, with snatches of conversation, random guitar and keyboard parts, a news broadcast and machine noise from an amusement arcade. These were compiled and inserted into the multi-track master, resulting in a short but mind-bending interlude and adding to the song's sense of strangeness. It's the sort of left-field nod that I've always loved on records, probably due to getting hooked on these very techniques via The Beatles' 'I Am The Walrus' when I was a 12-year-old back in 1967!

An instrumental mix of this track was included on the 2013 Esoteric CD reissue of the album, giving us a glimpse of the formative eight-track stage of its evolution before the later overdubs. It retains its enigmatic charm, even stripped down to Roland 808 drum machine, 12-string guitar and synthesizer washes.

Additional Material
'It's Not Easy' (Phillips, Scott)
This track replaced 'Exocet' when the UK version of the album was released in April 1984. It's a slow-paced plodder based around a steady drum box rhythm. Ant provides synths and guitars, as well as the lead vocal, while the song is beefed up by a brass section of Bimbo Acock (saxes, flute), Martin Drover (trumpet) and Malcolm Griffiths (trombone). Structurally, the song has a tuneful verse that builds in tense, emotional phrases as Ant ponders on the fact that breaking up is hard to do when you still retain strong feelings for someone. With his voice sounding at its most emotional, the taut verses release into the catchiness of a chorus that employs a chant of the song title. The chorus ends with the line, 'It's not easy, to face the light' – a shimmering synth chord underpins the word 'light'. There are occasional, soulful backing vocal interjections by Uti Koofreh on the choruses and chanting coda of the song and Joji Hirota decorates the rhythm track with various percussion instruments, including wood blocks, cowbell and darabukka, also known as a goblet drum – the national symbol of Egyptian Shabbi Music.

'Trail Of Tears' (Phillips, Scott)
This track first saw the light of day on the September 1985 compilation album *Harvest Of The Heart*. It was recorded in the spring of 1982 at

Englewood Studios but didn't make it onto the original release of *Invisible Men*. It has since appeared as an extra track on the CD reissues. The first section of this instrumental is driven by a slow-tempo drum box rhythm while the synthesized chord sequence works a well-worn, circulating four chords with a downbeat feel. After this lugubrious intro, the drum box unexpectedly gallops off rather clumsily into a sprightly tempo, while the synth lines also become more upbeat, with a sense of jollity to them. Unfortunately, the programming on this early drum machine struggles to cope with the increased tempo once some drum fills are attempted and the clattering results are almost comical. By the time drum machines evolved, they could get much closer to imitating real drum fills, but back in these early days, the limitations of these contraptions were highlighted by arrangements like this one. The two parts of this arrangement are played off one another, contrasting the slower, sombre sections with the upbeat, jollier melodies, but, in truth, it's easy to see why 'Trail Of Tears' didn't make the grade for the first choice of tracks for *Invisible Men*.

'The Ballad Of Penlee' (Phillips, Scott)
This song, however, would have made a worthy contender for consideration. Recorded at Englewood Studios in April 1983, it was remixed by Ant in October 1990 and appeared on later CD reissues. It is a simple but touching ballad that reflects on the Penlee lifeboat disaster, which occurred on 19 December 1981. Eight brave RNLI volunteers went to the aid of the MV Union Star as it foundered in heavy seas after its engines failed off the coast of Cornwall. Sadly, both vessels were lost, along with 16 lives. The arrangement of the song is wisely kept simple, with just Ant's piano backed with various keyboard sounds and Richard Scott's moving vocal. The chant of 'Solomon Brown' in the poignant choruses evokes the name of the lost lifeboat. The music is almost hymnal in its sad beauty, with the vocals following the piano line. It's a fitting tribute to the selfless souls who risk their own lives to save the lives of others around our coastline.

'Alex' (Phillips, Scott)
Another track that first emerged on the 1991 Virgin reissue in the form of a mix of the eight-track version recorded at Ant's studio, this was replaced by a mix from the Atmosphere Studios 24-track version on the 2017 Esoteric reissue. It remains instrumental in this form, bolstered by real drums from Jeff Dunne. Crying out to be furnished with lyrics, it has a song-like structure and proceeds at a medium pace. Ant plays the melody for the first section on electric guitar, contrasting a second section with a hymn-like vibe. Overall, it's a touching piece that would've been well worth working up as a finished track for the original album. Despite the fact it sounds somewhat incomplete without words, it's still exceptionally pleasant to listen to and makes a fine addition to the CD reissues.

'Gimme Love' (Phillips, Scott)

The second disc of the Esoteric Records 2017 CD reissue opens with the first of a selection of unfinished recordings in the pop-oriented style of *Invisible Men* that didn't make the final album. 'Gimme Love' is one of the more complete selections here and has a Richard Scott vocal. Recorded at Vic's Place in the spring of 1986, it was one of the demos for a potential second set of songs by the Phillips/Scott team. The drum programming is a basic 4/4 bass drum and clap rhythm, while Ant's Stratocaster plays some rhythmic chords against it in the style of Marc Bolan's rhythm guitar playing on the 1971 hit single 'Get It On', only slightly more laid back. The choruses display a pop brio; this was the era when Ant was dipping his toes into pop songwriting for the likes of Bucks Fizz. A certain Kitty Grant is credited with backing vocals, supporting Richard Scott's lead vocal. It's a more than decent pop tune.

'Mysterious Constitution Of Comets' (Phillips, Scott)

The next five tracks on disc two of the Esoteric reissue are all works in a certain amount of disrepair. This sequence, however, does evoke a hint of mystery, as a drum machine 'stick' sound underpins Ant's layered guitar picking over a chord scheme that feels as if something's going to occur at any minute, but it never quite does. Despite this, it has a great title, and combined with the vibe of the music, it had me cogitating on those fascinating wanderers of the solar system that brought fear and terror to earlier, more superstitious civilizations, who often regarded the appearance of a comet as a portent of doom! Of course, as every astronomer knows, the constitution of comets is that of a dirty snowball composed of rocks and ice, the latter evaporating as the comet moves nearer to the sun (hence the famous comet's tail).

'She's Gone' (Phillips, Scott)

Not the famous Hall & Oates ballad of the same name, but a Phillips/Scott original, 'She's Gone' is a basic backing track of Ant's guitars and keyboards over a drum box beat. Like many of these tracks, it feels incomplete and fails to hold the attention for too long.

'Graciella' (Phillips, Scott)

With its shuffling drum box and string chords, this tune displays good potential. It also features Jeremy Gilbert, who adds some basic harp plucking to the backing track.

'Over And Over Again' (Phillips, Scott)

Ant is on piano here in a pleasing sequence, building to a potential chorus where you can't help but sing the song's title over Ant's piano melody, as it fits the rhythm perfectly. Again, like many of these tracks, it's a shame the finished songs were never completed.

'Tonight' (Phillips, Scott)

This is the last of the handful of backing tracks remixed for the Esoteric release. Over a basic drum box, Ant plays some glowing synthesiser chords.

'Alien' (Phillips, Scott)

Recorded at Englewood studios in April 1983, 'Alien' at least boasts some Richard Scott vocals. The backing on this love song features Ant's spinet-like synth over a drum box beat as the big chorus moves to major from the more minor-tinged verses. It's a song that could've made the grade with a bit more polish.

'Refugee From Love' (Phillips, Scott)

Recorded at Englewood Studios in April 1983 and worked on again at Vic's Place in spring 1986, this song feels more complete and is a good example of the duo's penchant for upbeat pop songs. The chorus is very catchy, with its 'run away, run away' backing vocals, and would've really suited Bucks Fizz in the wake of Ant's tune 'Tears On The Ballroom Floor', co-written with songwriter Roy Hill, being included on the ex-Eurovision band's 1986 album *I Hear Talk*. Interestingly, he wasn't the only member of the progressive rock community writing for Bucks Fizz in the 1980s, as King Crimson's Pete Sinfield also co-wrote some of that group's biggest hits of the era.

'Something Blue' (Phillips, Scott)

This is a lovely tune, recorded at Englewood Studios in April 1983. Ant picks his acoustic guitar, backed with keyboard washes, as Richard Scott sings. The strength of this song's melody was underlined when Ant recorded an instrumental classical guitar solo version of this piece much later, in 1996, for his ninth *Private Parts & Pieces* album, *Dragonfly Dreams*.

'Holding You Again' (Phillips, Scott)

Another Englewood recording from April 1983, Ant's piano is backed with synths on this country-tinged ballad that found a productive afterlife as the key ballad from the Phillips/Scott musical *Alice*, staged at Leeds Playhouse in the spring of 1984 – more about this project in the next chapter.

'Darling' (Phillips, Scott)

One of the tracks that nearly made it onto the original album, 'Darling' is a nifty triple-time tune on which Ant plays some effective slides on his guitar and contributes some picking on his mandocello. The distinctive accordion breaks were played by session man Jack Emblow and are sonically similar in feel to the whimsical accordion-like breaks on The Beach Boys' 'Fall Breaks And Back To Winter (W. Woodpecker Symphony)' from their 1967 album *Smiley Smile*. Emblow is perhaps most famous for his accordion contribution to The Beatles' 1967 hit single 'All You Need Is Love'. For me, he's equally respected for the cascading accordion runs that graced the ebullient 1973 Stackridge single 'The Galloping Gaucho'.

'Shadow In The Desert' (Phillips, Scott)
This triple-time, drum box-driven backing track is a moodier affair with a prominent bass synthesiser and a descending synth sequence combined with more staccato synth chords. The bass synth returns later, along with some jiggling synth notes. It was initially recorded at Englewood, transferring to Atmosphere by the autumn of 1982. There is some piano audible in the mix, but, in truth, it just feels like a further backing track awaiting completion.

'Finale' (Phillips)
One of Ant's solo compositions, this was presumably intended to wrap up the *Invisible Men* album but had to wait until 2004 before it first saw the light of day on the *Archive Collection Volume Two* CD. It closes the second disc of the 2017 Esoteric CD reissue and does at least boast a real drummer in the shape of Paul Robinson. Still feeling a tad incomplete to my ears, it employs a kind of circling sequence, building to some big synth chords. Best of all here, though, is Ant's electric guitar as he cuts loose for some soloing, which is always a pleasure to listen to.

'Duchess Of Kew' (Phillips)
This recording didn't turn up until the 2015 release of the CD *Private Parts & Extra Pieces*, but it was recorded at Englewood Studios in the spring of 1982 as a potential candidate for *Invisible Men*. With Richard Scott on the Roland 808 drum box and Ant playing keyboards and guitars, the 12-strings are panned out to either side of the mix and play complementary parts as the drum box provides the slowly moving rhythm. Some piping synthesiser makes an appearance. It's an agreeable chord sequence that feels a tad incomplete.

Anthony Phillips 1977-1990 ... *On Track*

Private Parts & Pieces IV: A Catch At The Tables (1984)

Personnel:

Anthony Phillips: 12-string guitar, six-string guitar, Rudloff eight-string guitar, Polymoog, ARP 2600 synthesiser, Mellotron, charango, Roland 808 drum box

Mark Emney: bugle ('Sistine')

Judd Lander: bagpipes, harmonica ('Sistine')

Recorded: Send Barns, Englewood, Vic's Place and Atmosphere Studios, 1979-1982

Producer: Anthony Phillips, except 'Sistine', produced by Anthony Phillips, Richard Scott and Trevor Vallis

Artwork: Elsworth

Mastered at Townhouse Studios by Ian 'that sounds bloody awful' Cooper, September 1983

Record label: Passport (US)

Released: April 1984, Passport (US); CD rerelease, Virgin, 1991; CD rerelease, Blueprint, 1996; CD rerelease with Private Parts And Pieces III, Voiceprint, February 2012; CD rerelease as part of Private Parts And Pieces I-IV, Esoteric, September 2015

More of a compilation album than the third *Private Parts & Pieces* release, *A Catch At The Tables* pretty much mopped up the remaining Send Barns recordings made between 1979 and 1982. One of my own personal favourites of the series, it's also an album that presents a varied selection of styles: classical-styled guitar pieces, synthesiser improvisations and even one of Ant's finest songs of the period, 'Sistine' – another escapee from the *Invisible Men* sessions of 1982.

By the time *A Catch At The Tables* was released in April 1984, Ant's second attempt at a stage musical, *Alice*, co-written with Richard Scott, had started its run at Leeds Playhouse. It's a shame there was no album release in connection with this show, as it's a work that highlights the range of Ant's songwriting, taking in ballads, 1920s pastiches and bluesy cabaret-style songs. Happily, I have an audience cassette recording of a performance of this stage show in my collection to remind me of its qualities. Ant spoke at length about *Alice* in a two-part interview printed in *Genesis Magazine* (Issue No. 31, dated April 1984, and Issue No.32, dated summer 1984). His vocal tutor, John Owen Edwards, was heavily involved in preparing the music for staging, along with Musical Performance Director Kevin Fitzsimmons, and the whole thing was a big success at the time. The rumours were that if it made it to the West End of London, an album might be considered, but although it did well regionally, this never came to pass. Some of the material for Ant's former abandoned project, *Masquerade*, was recycled into *Alice*. The musical was so called as it was loosely based on Lewis Carroll's *Alice In Wonderland* but transferred into a more modern technological setting. It proved to be a project that stretched

76

Ant musically and he learnt a lot about working to deadlines and combining music with other media from it, lessons he put to good use over his extensive library and soundtrack work spread throughout his long career.

Again, there was no UK release for *A Catch At The Tables*, so it was only available on import again in the UK via its US release on Passport Records. The artwork this time wasn't by Peter Cross but was a rather atmospheric painting by Elsworth picturing a Victorian boating party out on a lake. It was rendered in shades of purple with a misty shoreline in the background. The reverse cover consisted of the album credits surrounded by angling imagery.

'Arboretum Suite' (Phillips)
Recorded at Send Barns in July 1980, this opening suite is constructed of four short movements. The arboretum in question is at Winkworth, near Godalming in Surrey. Ant originally wrote this suite for the wedding of his friends Chris and Jackie Maliphant.

The first movement, 'Set Piece', is described by Ant as 'a slightly Spanish-flavoured allegro'. It's a fast triple-time guitar piece that fairly gallops along, contrasting speedy arpeggios – accompanied by plentiful fret squeaks – with slower chording. It makes a sprightly start to this charming suite.

The second movement, 'Over The Gate', moves to a slower, pastoral feel and has a lovely rising melody. In Ant's words, it's a 'dreamy largo' and I would heartily concur with his description. Two 12-string guitars are involved, one slightly sped-up, along with Polymoog and ARP 2600 chording, but best of all are the interludes of picking on Ant's eight-string Rudloff guitar. An alternate mix of this section was later included on the CD *Private Parts & Extra Pieces*.

The jaunty 'Flapjack' makes for a spirit-raising third movement. This is a short but playful classical guitar duet with a sense of mischief about it. Later CD reissues also presented a solo classical guitar version of this movement as one of the bonus tracks.

The suite closes with a reflective fourth movement, 'Lights On The Hill', underpinned by a slow, discreet drum box rhythm. The 12-string guitar is joined by a John Bailey six-string, and later in the piece, Polymoog and ARP 2600 synthesisers play a series of poignant chords, bringing the suite to a suitably elegiac conclusion. Ant also drops in some gorgeous runs on his Ovation bass guitar around the 3.33 mark. It's a piece that evolved from one of the songs that Ant had worked up with Richard Scott for the aborted *Masquerade* project, which subsequently became a number employed in the duo's *Alice* musical under the title 'Walls And Bridges'. It's a sequence that would reappear as the coda of the track, 'A Catch At The Tables', one of the bonus treats added to later CD reissues of *Private Parts & Pieces IV*.

'Earth Man' (Phillips)
This Polymoog improvisation was recorded in October 1979 at Send Barns and evinces a strong sci-fi feel with its bass note underpin and ominous

chording. Its slow and moody atmosphere adds to the balance of an album that contrasts composed music with improvisatory tracks like this one. Sometimes, spontaneous recordings that rely on serendipity and instant inspiration can often provide the most exciting musical moments of all. Equally, they can also quite as easily fall flat on a less inspired day. This track, however, is well worth inclusion and makes an effective contrast piece to the varied selection of musical styles presented on this album.

'Dawn Over The Lake' (Phillips)
Rather more ponderous is this 12-string guitar and drum box improvisation ('in a long-forgotten tuning' according to Ant's sleeve notes). Recorded at Send Barns in March 1981, it starts with a touch of 12-string harmonics before proceeding to more relaxed 12-string arpeggio picking. The thing I like best about this recording is the subtle deployment of repeat echoes on various instruments – even the fret squeaks on the 12-string sound mesmerising when treated in this way! Personally, I'm a sucker for this sort of recording technique, and for me, it rescues this rather lengthy improvisation as a listening experience. Running for an inordinate 10.55, it's a track that's best appreciated by those listeners with a 12-string guitar obsession or those, like me, who are fascinated by the employment of repeat echo on recordings!

'Bouncer' (Phillips)
Shorter but more violent is this sledgehammer drum box-powered trifle, bashed out by Ant during the sessions for the *Invisible Men* album at Englewood Studios in June 1982 while he was waiting for producer Trevor Vallis to turn up. There's a touch of menace to Ant's rhythmic 12-string figures and the track comes to a sudden, sharp ending after 3.05, providing a bracing start to side two.

'Eduardo' (Phillips)
Recorded at Send Barns in August 1981, this solo guitar excursion by Ant, played on his eight-string Rudloff, provides an early highlight on side two. Described as an 'Italian-flavoured ramble' by its author, to my ears, this is a brilliant classical guitar composition executed fingerstyle with enviable technical skill. Played in C#, the opening melody, descending from the note G#, plays off a repeating lower note of C#, creating a pedal effect behind the lead line. C# isn't the easiest guitar key to play in without a neck capo, but Ant makes it sound like a stroll in the park. We're treated to some lively triplet-based, up-and-down runs taken a high speed, and although the piece runs for a lengthy 9.53, it more than justifies its length via a series of modulations and developments that explore the possibilities laid out in the early part of the composition. These move through arpeggios, faster staccato chording and delicate fingerstyle picking sections, always developing the piece organically as the styles change throughout. There's a tidy recapitulation

of the opening theme towards the close of the piece, completing one of Ant's best solo guitar outings.

'Heart Of Darkness' (Phillips)
Recorded at Send Barns in September 1980, this churchy-sounding mood piece played on Polymoog and Mellotron was described as 'concerto grotto-style' by Ant in his sleeve notes. Descending waves of Polymoog chords create a forbidding atmosphere, reflecting the title of the piece, possibly influenced by the famous 1899 Joseph Conrad novella of the same name. A lone Mellotron flute enters the picture at 1.20, extemporising on the melody. It proves to be an effective combination of keyboards, and between 3.07 and 3.10, there are some particularly lovely Mellotron flute figures.

'The Sea And The Armadillo' (Phillips)
Ant's aquatic 12-string is joined by two Ovation six-string guitars in the first half of this recording, laid down at Send Barns in August 1981. A twiddly five-note guitar phrase is answered by strumming chords, the first section presumably representing the sea. At 3.21, the armadillo arrives on the scene, conjured by the rhythmic strumming of an Andean stringed instrument of the lute family, known as a charango. By the close of play, there are two of these instruments scrubbing away and the sleeve notes credit the charango playing to one Pedro Luigi Crass (more than likely another pseudonym for Ant!). Amusingly, the sleeve also bears the legend, 'Armadillo trained by Ralph Bernascone'.

'Sistine' (Phillips)
Started at the sessions for *Invisible Men* at Englewood Studios in June 1982 and surprisingly not selected for the album at the time, this is simply one of Ant's most glorious songs. It was completed at Atmosphere Studios in September of that year and was thankfully chosen to close *Private Parts & Pieces IV*. While on a visit to Rome, Ant had a flash of inspiration in the Sistine Chapel and scribbled out the song's lyrics on someone's calling card. From the whooshing sound in the intro, this recording is a slice of pure magic. A delicate reverb-treated piano line introduces the verse melody, its cathedral-like sound enhancing the moving lyrics – the whole thing is perfectly titled.

The subject is a serviceman shipping out to a war zone (again, possibly influenced by the Falklands' conflict of the time). In the chorus, the soldier attempts to reassure his loved one that he'll be home soon. Combined with the moving melody of its memorable verse/chorus, the lyrics are deeply moving, while the extraordinary musical arrangement features the most perfect touches along the way. The key modulation at 2.00 is positively heart-lifting and the instrumental interlude midway through the song sounds sublime thanks to Judd Lander's bagpipes and harmonica. Lander was the go-to session harmonica player during the 1980s and was soon to be famous for the addition of his distinctive harmonica contribution to Culture Club's 1983 hit single 'Karma Chameleon'.

The finishing touch to 'Sistine', which I regard as Ant's most perfect song, arrives with a classic turnaround in the final chorus, while Mark Emney's contribution on bugle is another inspired brushstroke to a song that's positively hymnal in its poignancy and is proof positive of Ant's considerable songwriting skills. It's an utterly wonderful recording.

Additional Material
'Erotic Strings' (Phillips)
Recorded at Vic's Place in January 1985, 'Erotic Strings' is a short but climactic instrumental. It was first released on the compilation album *Harvest Of The Heart* on Cherry Red Records in September 1985. It reappeared as a bonus track on the later CD rereleases of *Private Parts & Pieces IV*. Originally, it was employed as incidental music for the Limehouse Productions play *Tropical Moon Over Dorking*, starring Pauline Collins and Michael Gambon, which was broadcast on Channel 4 on 31 March 1985, with a repeat broadcast on 13 December 1986.

Performed mainly on synthesisers, it showcases an ever-ascending cascade of sound that, rather fittingly considering the title, rises to a climax after 1.08 – short but satisfying indeed!

'A Catch At The Tables' (Phillips)
Another rather short acoustic guitar piece added to the CD reissues, the belated title track consists of some interesting arpeggio picking in 7/8 time before moving to a reprise of the sequence from the last movement of 'Arboretum Suite', 'Lights On The Hill', after 2.24, making a conceptual link with the parent album.

'Theme From Operation Whale' (Phillips)
Something of an odd track out, this solo guitar version of the theme from the Greenpeace film documentary *Operation Whale* was recorded at Send Barns in August 1980. The film covers an attempt by Greenpeace's converted trawler, 'Rainbow Warrior', to disrupt the slaughter of whales in Icelandic waters between 1978 and 1980. Unfortunately, the Greenpeace ship would meet a sad end in the event of the sinking of the vessel by French foreign intelligence agents during Greenpeace's attempted disruption to French nuclear tests in the South Pacific on 10 July 1985.

On this version of the *Operation Whale* theme, Ant combines arpeggios with faster runs, moving his picking hand towards and away from the bridge of the guitar, thus varying the tone from softer to more brittle where required. Again, it's a track that was added to later CD reissues of *Private Parts & Pieces IV*.

'Prelude 3' (Phillips)

This classical guitar piece was from one of the last Send Barns' sessions, recorded in August 1981. Its slow chordal strum moves through a downbeat sequence with a distinct sinking feeling to it before moving to a higher octave as it develops. It was first released on the CD *Private Parts & Extra Pieces* in 2015.

'Sea Sketches' (Phillips)

A variation on the themes of 'The Sea And The Armadillo', this interesting 12-string composition was recorded at Send Barns in August 1981. Its guitar arpeggios double up as Ant's fingers dance impressively over his 12-string fretboard. It has an interesting chord structure that, at 3.12, moves back to the initial variations but remains very much with the sea: the armadillo will return shortly, no doubt after Mr Bernascone has completed its training!

'Armadillo Air' (Phillips)

And here it is, fresh from training, as we join our rather jaunty armadillo, conjured via two chunky-sounding charangos played by Ant but sounding a dead ringer for George Formby's rhythmic style on banjolele: 'Eh, it's turned out nice again!'

Private Parts & Pieces V: Twelve (1985)

Personnel:
Anthony Phillips: Alvarez 12-string guitar
Recorded: Englewood Studios, September 1984
Producer: Anthony Phillips
Cut by Ian Cooper at Townhouse, London and Greg Calbi, Sterling Sound, NYC
Artwork: Peter Cross (front cover); Murray Brenman (back cover)
Record label: Passport (US)
Released: 17 January 1985, Passport (US); CD rerelease, Virgin, 1991; CD rerelease, Blueprint, 1996; CD rerelease with Private Parts & Pieces VI, Voiceprint, May 2010; CD rerelease, Esoteric as part of Private Parts & Pieces V-VIII, September 2016

It had to happen at some point. A whole album dedicated to the instrument perhaps most associated with Ant: the 12-string guitar. From his pioneering work, along with partner Mike Rutherford, on the early Genesis recordings, Ant has always been the consummate explorer of 12-string possibilities. From unusual inversions to exotic tunings, through harmonic layering to graphic manipulation of its sound, Ant has experimented fearlessly with his beloved 12-string through the years. Here, then, is a suite that matches the 12 strings of the guitar to the 12 months of the year. The seasons have always provided a potent symbol for artists throughout the centuries: Antonio Vivaldi's suite of concerti, *The Four Seasons,* springs to mind, and in popular music, many examples abound, from XTC's 'Season Cycle' to The Enid's 1984 classic progressive rock album *The Spell*, which equates the four seasons to a human lifetime. Ant keeps the concept simple, using the calendar months as titles for each piece, starting and ending in northern hemisphere winter, moving from January to December. Unlike many of the earlier *Private Parts & Pieces* albums (apart from *Antiques*), *Twelve* is a complete project rather than a compilation of older recordings, giving it a strong conceptual coherence. It's true to say that it's a more testing listening experience for the casual listener, concentrating as it does on the one instrument, but for aficionados of the 12-string, it's an absolute beanfeast!

This is indeed a true solo album, recorded by Ant in his own Englewood Studios and self-produced. The enigmatic Mr Bernascone gets a mention on the sleeve credits, with the legend: 'Inspired by Ralph Bernascone's operetta '12 Vodka Night''! Originally envisaged as an orchestral album, a lack of funding and time constraints resulted in a simpler solution being sought – hence a 12-string guitar album. The serendipitous discovery of an unusual guitar tuning found Ant adopting it for this album, adding to the record's distinctive ambience of plentiful open strings.

Peter Cross returns once more to provide the front cover artwork in his marvellously detailed and humorous way. Reflecting the concept of the title, each month is depicted visually via 12 small paintings in a clock-like circular ring, with lots of subtle jocularity in the detail of the portraits, including allusions to the *Twelve* concept and caricatures relating to Ant and his manager, Tony Smith. The names of the months are inscribed around the edge in Latin. Like all of Cross's work, it's great fun to peruse at leisure whilst listening to the album. The reverse of the album features a round, soft-focus colour photo of Ant cradling his 12-string guitar, with the credits printed on the white background of the sleeve.

When I located my vinyl copy of this album, in preparation for a reassessment of it for this book, I realised that in the 40 years since I eagerly obtained my import copy of *Twelve*, I'd probably only listened to it in its entirety a handful of times. This is often the case with me (and I suspect many others) when an album focuses on a single instrument. This often leads to a lack of tonal variation that, when listened to in one sitting, proves much more demanding on a listener's concentration. It's true to say that this is, therefore, one of Ant's most neglected and least celebrated album releases; hard to digest in a single listen, the tracks possibly shine out more when listened to in isolation from the parent album, where the contrast stands out more clearly against other styles of music. It may well be more an album for Ant completists than the casual listener, but nevertheless, it's time to give it a go and explore the changing seasons in the company of one man and his 12-string guitar.

'January' (Phillips)
Ironically enough for northern hemisphere dwellers, the point of perihelion – Planet Earth's closest approach to the sun during its 365-and-a-quarter day orbit around our parent star – occurs in January, when the northern hemisphere is at its coldest. It's the Earth's axial tilt of 23-and-a-half degrees that gives rise to the seasons rather than the planet's proximity to the sun. Here, Ant reflects the coldest season in the north by introducing a lonely five-note motif and some arpeggio picking from high to low. The music takes on a curious oriental feel in places, and a flurry of arpeggios midway through suggests snowfall. A faster triplet feel in the second half of the piece, with some rising chords, occurs before a return to the five-note motif.

'February' (Phillips)
Still often a chilly, unpredictable month for us northerners, 'February' comes in with some vacillating chords that soon transform into a creeping theme, suggestive of furtive footsteps in the snow. The piece moves to some higher chordal picking before a return to the vacillating chords that opened it. This section, at times, suggests the feel of the slow ticking theme from the opening part of Gustav Holst's 'Saturn: The Bringer Of Old Age' from *The Planets' Suite*.

'March' (Phillips)
Some dancing arpeggios here suggest hints of spring approaching as we negotiate the vernal equinox (when day and night are of equal length). Ant's

12-string picking increases in speed, suggesting March winds as it lifts towards some guitar harmonics.

'April' (Phillips)
With its sunshine and showers, the unpredictability of April is reflected here with bell-like tones, Ant's playing moving from brittle to dampened with a picking feel very much like *The Geese & The Ghost*. 'April' is the most dynamically active track so far and some of the rhythmic chordal scrubbing here sounds quite energetic!

'May' (Phillips)
The previous month's sunshine and showers bring forth May flowers that bloom here via a four-note and a six-note motif separated by a rest bar. The progression of the piece then expands on this theme, displaying an organic development mainly based in G#. Interestingly, the month is named after the Greek goddess of fertility, Maia – May is also a month of significance in pagan folk culture – hence the Morris and Maypole dancing of English folk music.

'June' (Phillips)
The month of the summer solstice in the northern hemisphere, flaming June, is represented here with a combination of rising chords and rhythmic strumming. There is a mere hint in the 12-string chording here of George Harrison's 'Here Comes The Sun' from the 1969 Beatles album *Abbey Road*. Whether this is subconscious or intended is uncertain, but it's a fitting nod to the evocation of a month which we trust will be blessed with sunshine.

'July' (Phillips)
Named for Roman emperor Julius Caesar, the month of July introduces the dog days of summer, when Sirius, the 'Dog Star', first becomes visible again in the morning skies. Ant reflects on the onset of the northern hemisphere's hottest period with a 12-string composition that sets out with a series of punctuating chords followed by short, picked phrases. This intro settles into an engaging triple-time dancing melody that is almost song-like in structure before moving to slower variations on a theme. A reflective passage in triple time calms the atmosphere prior to a further burst of rhythmic chording. Towards the close of the track, tinkling arpeggios perhaps evoke an unpredictable summer shower before a brief return to the dancing melody heard earlier.

'August' (Phillips)
Single notes and picked harmonics collide with rhythmic phrases and arpeggio picking on a piece representing what is often the hottest month for northern hemisphere dwellers. There is a distinct wandering feel to proceedings here in a track that lacks a strong identity. Of interest are some rhythmic 'chukkas'

played by Ant using dampening, and there's also a peculiar shimmering effect that he drags from his 12-string towards the end of the piece.

'September' (Phillips)

Ant's playing is noticeably spikier in the intro to this drifting tribute to the month of the autumnal equinox and harvesting. Among the triple-time arpeggios, there is a descending sequence of chords that possibly represent the fall of autumn leaves as the summer fades. The piece moves to slower 4/4 time towards the end.

'October' (Phillips)

Ant's 12-string chords here sound both mysterious and lonely in this ruminative evocation of October. There are some nice variations of accenting in his playing, from tasty fingerpicking to slow chordal picking, with occasional harmonics thrown in. The odd shimmering we heard back in 'August' also makes a return, adding to the track's sense of mystery. This is also the track where, during a particularly quiet passage, Ant's lodger of the time, Edward Cooper, left the premises with a loud slam of the front door – see if you can hear it. It gained Mr Cooper the credit, 'Front door on 'October': 'Crocodile' Cooper', on the rear sleeve of *Twelve* at the time!

'November' (Phillips)

For a month I always tend to associate with fog, Ant's 'November' is an extremely active and dynamic composition. Opening with dampened guitar riffs, there is a brief excursion into 7/4 time and the dampened riffs are contrasted with highly rhythmic chording that, at times, sounds quite violent, with Ant showing little mercy as he attacks his 12-string with gusto. One of the more demonstrative tracks on the album, I'm attracted to this piece by its rhythmic content – perhaps I relate to it more, as I'm an enthusiastic exponent of rhythm guitar myself. The rhythmic pounding is contrasted by some equally manic riffs darting about at high speed like a demented wasp! It ends with a heavily rhythmic build-up and some scrubbed chords, with a final bout of manic riffing to close.

'December' (Phillips)

After the drama of the previous month, 'December' sounds positively frigid as Ant explores a chilly-sounding sequence. It's a more reflective conjuring of the month of the winter solstice in the northern hemisphere. A rhythmic section accents three chords against a four-chord phrase, but it's all less dynamic than the track that preceded it. Some crystalline picking, chiming against a pedal effect, brings things towards a close.

It's true to say *Twelve* demands a commitment on the part of the listener, and for that reason, it is certainly Ant's least commercial album up to this point. But his artistic integrity in embarking on and securing release for an album solely of solo 12-string pieces, appealing mainly to hardcore fans, is admirable. It's certainly no surprise that, back in 1985, this album was only available in the UK on import.

Private Parts & Pieces VI: Ivory Moon (1986)

Personnel:
Anthony Phillips: piano
Recorded: Englewood Studios, London, August 1985
Producer: Anthony Phillips
Cut by Ian Cooper at Townhouse Studios, London
Artwork: Peter Cross
Record label: Passport (US)
Released: January 1986, Passport (US); CD rerelease, Virgin, 1991; CD rerelease, Blueprint, 1996; CD rerelease with Private Parts & Pieces V, Voiceprint, May 2010, CD rerelease as part of Private Parts & Pieces V-VIII, Esoteric, September 2016

Subtitled 'Piano Pieces 1971-1985', this addition to the *Private Parts & Pieces* series does indeed concentrate on Ant 'tickling the ivories' on a selection of his own piano compositions from the previous 14 years, performed and recorded at his studio, Englewood, during August 1985. The month after Ant recorded this album, the excellent compilation album *Harvest Of The Heart* was released on Cherry Red Records, highlighting a well-chosen selection of tracks from the first four editions of the *Private Parts & Pieces* series, along with several tracks that were previously unavailable at the time: 'Trail Of Tears' and 'Erotic Strings'.

Ivory Moon again sports artwork by Peter Cross in the form of an impression of Leith Hill Tower, near Dorking (one of Ant's local landmarks in his early years), with various caricatures around its entrance, including Ant's manager Tony Smith and Ant himself chasing a frisbee down a hill. Several dogs are pictured with the humans, the painting being titled 'Sea-Dogs Motoring' – which is also the name of the opening suite on the album. Alongside Cross's artwork, the album title, *Ivory Moon*, along with Ant's name, is written from top to bottom in an oriental-style font on a cream background. The reverse side of the cover has the credits printed on the top left and a colour photo of Ant in cricketing whites at the bottom right of the rear sleeve. Like several others of the series, *Ivory Moon* was initially only available in the UK as a US import. The mysterious Ralph Bernascone makes an appearance in the credits thus: 'Ralph Bernascone appears curtesy (*sic*) of Ravaged Records' and Ant's piano tuner, John Armer, gets a mention as well!

It's true to say that the proviso for Ant's previous *Private Parts & Pieces* album, *Twelve*, goes for *Ivory Moon,* too. For those who struggle to maintain concentration whilst listening to albums dedicated to only one instrument, this may pose a problem. However, for those who love the sound of a piano, this album is a dream scenario. For piano fans, there is much to love here, as Ant performs this selection of favoured piano pieces from his own *oeuvre*.

'Suite: Sea-Dogs Motoring' (Phillips)

This four-piece suite is based on Peter Cross's cover painting of the same name. The salty sea dogs in question awake early for the first movement: 'Sunrise Over Sienna'. This scene is conjured via a combination of strident piano chords and more peaceful interludes with occasional florid upward runs. For this composition, Ant was influenced by the style of Italian classical composer Ottorino Respighi (1879-1936). The piano is nicely recorded and the piece builds in intensity, only to subside back to tinkling runs on the treble end of the piano, rather fittingly, like the ebb and flow of the tide.

The second section, 'Basking Shark', is also perfectly descriptive, as staccato chords are very soon underpinned by a series of piano bass notes that march around beneath the chords, emanating a sense of menace a la *Jaws*. The same stalking pattern migrates to a higher octave as our fishy fiend circles its unsuspecting prey. Some spreading piano arpeggios like lapping waves soon have supporting harmony notes moving beneath them, then following them, as we get the feeling our shark has progressed from basking to thinking about a hearty lunch. Several discreet modulations move the urgency of the music up a notch or two, along with a degree of *accelerando* as our peckish predator prepares to move in for the kill. At this point, the shark appears to change its mind as we return to the original marching bass notes. Some big, concerto-like piano chords lead to a series of lightning-fast piano runs – perhaps illustrating our sea dogs swimming for their life as the stalking bass notes represent the shark attempting pursuit.

The third section, 'Sea-Dogs Air', finds our survivors jigging with joy as we move into a delightful triple-time movement overlaid by a speedy figure, evincing a distinctly nautical air. There's some strong melodic development as the music modulates, with lots of tinkling runs on display. We again accelerate towards the close of this section, restating the air heard earlier, and the piece is capped by a whimsical ending, climaxing in a dead stop.

The final section of the suite is named 'Safe Havens' as, after the dancing jubilation of avoiding becoming the basking shark's midday meal, our sea dogs settle for a relaxing afternoon in the sun, as peaceful piano chords reflect the last section's title. All in all, 'Suite: Sea-Dogs Motoring' makes for an impressive and adventuresome start to Ant's first solo piano album.

'Tara's Theme' (from *Masquerade*) (Phillips)

With a working title of 'Riddles', 'Tara's Theme' is another refugee from the *Masquerade* project, which had been based on Kit Williams' armchair treasure hunt book of the same name, published in August 1979. The piece evinces a bold romanticism in its rising and falling melody lines over steadily moving left-hand arpeggios. Like some grand theme from an epic imaginary movie, undulating chords underpin a melody that, to my ears, has a tangential relationship with Ant's earlier song, 'Lucy: An Illusion', in that both that song and 'Tara's Theme' hint at the melody of the well-covered standard, 'It's All In The Game' (see chapter on *Private Parts & Pieces II: Back To The Pavilion*).

'Winter's Thaw' (Phillips)

This is a piece influenced by the lack of insulation in Ant's parents' house, which, back in the day, resulted in him wearing mittens whilst playing the piano in his room during the coldest months of winter! Parts of this impressionistic piano piece were composed as far back as 1971. Opening with slow, two-to-the-bar chords, 'Winter's Thaw' builds as slowly as a dripping icicle in the early morning sunshine. The slow melt is evoked by the gentle progression of piano notes towards the treble end of the instrument. The movement to triple time reflects the ever-increasing thaw as the sun rises higher in the sky. The flow of the piece is perfectly descriptive of this process as Ant moves the action to some higher arpeggios, followed by faster semiquaver runs like rivulets of flowing liquid. A move back to the initial slower chording is temporary, as we're soon back to mazy runs with both left and right hands and an almost Semprini-style build-up, incorporating Ant's usual logic as the piece develops. More florid runs towards the treble end of the keyboard eventually recede back to slow chording to complete side one of *Ivory Moon* on a contemplative note.

'The Old House' (Phillips)

This musical portrait of an old house opens with a series of slow-paced, steadily moving bass-end piano notes accompanied by chinking chord work. Moving to a higher octave, Ant plays a series of trailing chords in fast single notes moving from left to right on the keyboard as his hands lightly trip over the keys, while some wandering, independent notes at the bass end support the ringing treble chording. The slower contemplation returns as we make our way around the old house in question until some speedy, higher-octave semiquavers raise the vision of scurrying mice under the floorboards. Some dramatic bass-end triplets move to grander, concerto-like chording as the piece demonstrates an impressive build. Heavier, triplet-based staccato chords lead us to a slowly wandering interlude on the deeper notes while Ant negotiates a slow, chinking melody with his right hand.

A degree of *accelerando* gives 'The Old House' an organically moving flow as faster arpeggios lead into a notable downward run at the treble end into a more reflective passage that sounds positively filmic. An impressive big chord run up and down the keyboard leads into some slower chords topped by short, flowery runs on the higher notes with fast, spreading right-hand figures. Warmer-sounding chords that feel like sunshine through an old, broken windowpane introduce another variation as our journey around this old house points us towards the exit. With a warmer, romantic feel to the music, it feels as if we're perhaps viewing the old building from the outside, taking in its antiquated charm. This gentler interlude has a nice set of changes, as its skilful modulations head us towards a close. There is just time for a reprise of the big chord-run up and down the keyboard, as encountered earlier in the piece, before heading home via some higher octave doodles, completing our lengthy journey of 15.17.

'Moonfall' (from *Masquerade*) (Phillips, Hine)
This is a collaboration by Ant with the multi-talented Rupert Hine, who was well involved in the original *Masquerade* project, from which this is another musical example. Its song-like structure displays steady movement combined with melodious cascades at the treble end. Another piece that sounds wildly romantic, it builds up grandly around the halfway point and features distinctive employment of descending two-note piano figures at the higher octave, lending the piece a prepossessing charm. Again, it's all rather grand and cinematic and makes a good contrast with the more intense compositions that surround it. The music from the *Masquerade* project will be more fully discussed in a later chapter, as it was eventually made available via the Esoteric Records five-CD set *Archive Collection Volume I & Volume II* in 2022.

An earlier version of 'Moonfall' can be found on the CD *Private Parts & Extra Pieces II*, which is included with Esoteric Records' 2016 rerelease of *Private Parts & Pieces V-VIII*. This earlier version was composed entirely by Ant before Rupert Hine's composing contribution was added for the *Ivory Moon* recording.

'Rapids' (Phillips)
The vinyl version of *Ivory Moon* closes with this impressionistic piano piece that follows the course of a rock-strewn river on its downhill journey, judging by the title. Some tumbling notes and slower chording see us set off on our downhill journey. There are some effective modulations as we traverse the river's course, the flow slowly building up. After a while, a triple-time flow moves us downstream as spreading bass-end notes introduce a faster passage of semiquavers, indicating the rapids in question are about to be negotiated.

All then slows up just before the composition's halfway point as a steadily moving tempo ushers in a more becalmed mode. There is a further burst of faster movement around the 5.20 mark until all moves back to a calmer mode with smaller eddies of sound, eventually becoming a slowly burbling stream by the closing 8.25 mark.

Additional Material
'Let Us Now Make Love' (Phillips)
A welcome bonus track on the CD reissues of *Ivory Moon*, recorded by Ant at Vic's Place in October 1990, is this instrumental piano version of a Genesis song, written entirely by Ant during the 1969-1970 Christmas Cottage rehearsal sessions that found Genesis finally getting to grips with their collective muse after the schoolboy naivety of their first album, *From Genesis*

To Revelation. A popular and valued feature of the Genesis set during their 1969-1970 gigs, 'Let Us Now Make Love' was under consideration for inclusion on the band's 1970 album *Trespass* and was only held back as it was a strong contender for single release. Once Ant left Genesis in July 1970, the band dropped the song from their setlist. On stage, Peter Gabriel provided vocals and flute, Ant, along with Mike Rutherford, played 12-string guitars, while Tony Banks played organ and borrowed Ant's Fender Stratocaster for the instrumental sections, where the guitar was put through a Leslie speaker. It proved a popular number with their early audiences, and when Genesis played a gig at Queen Mary College in Mile End, East London on 4 February 1970, no less a personage than singer/songwriter Nick Drake (more obscure in 1970, but posthumously something of a legend) approached Ant, enquiring about the song's composer. As Ant proudly announced his authorship of the song, Drake gave his verdict on it by uttering 'Dangerous!' – I take it he was impressed!

Ant's piano version pretty much stays faithful to the Genesis arrangement and brings out the melodiousness of the tune. The only absent arrangement touch is Peter Gabriel's 'Polly Put The Kettle On' flute riff (which he also employed on 'The Musical Box', something of a party piece, I guess!). The Genesis version, recorded for *BBC Nightride* on 22 February 1970, can be located on the *Genesis Archive 1967-1975* box set.

Private Parts & Pieces VII: Slow Waves, Soft Stars (1987)

Personnel:

Anthony Phillips: Roland Jupiter 8, Casio 5000, ARP 2600 Polymoog, Yari classical guitar, Rudloff eight-string guitar, Alvarez 12-string guitar, Tom drum machine, Tibetan bells and chimes, zither

Enrique Berro Garcia: classical guitar ('Beachrunner', 'End Of The Affair')

Ralph Bernascone: frying pan ('Bubble & Squeak')

Recorded: Englewood Studios, Clapham, London, July 1983 – March 1987

Technical supervision: Paul Graves

Producer: Anthony Phillips

Artwork: Murray Brenman

Front cover photography: Vic Stench of Thrombosis

Back cover photography: Tif Hunter

Record label: Audion (US)

Released: 7 August 1987, Audion (US); CD rerelease, Virgin, 1991; CD rerelease, Blueprint, 1996; CD rerelease with New England, Voiceprint, May 2010; CD rerelease as part of Private Parts & Pieces V-VIII, Esoteric, September 2016

Slow Waves, Soft Stars is an album that neatly mops up some of the more interesting short compositions and improvisatory doodles accumulated by Ant over the previous four years. It's his seventh *Private Parts & Pieces* collection in eight years and the third on the trot without a main sequence release in between. His continued record company hassles again meant no UK release, meaning its availability in his home country was once more on import only.

Peter Cross wasn't involved with the cover artwork this time as Murray Brenman worked up a design, which is dominated by two photos: the front cover picture is credited to Ant's pseudonymous counterpart, Vic Stench, but was, in fact, snapped by Ant on a trip to Portugal using the wrong exposure. It's still an evocative photo of our own star, the sun, in a darkling sky over the sea off the Portuguese coastline. The photo is set on a green background and is surrounded by countless tiny waves in black. The photo of Ant on the reverse of the cover again shows him in cricketing whites, cradling a cricket ball. It was taken by Tif Hunter using a fisheye lens whilst on a boat trip to France in 1981.

'Ice Flight' (Phillips)

Private Parts & Pieces VII floats in with a five-part suite reflecting the frozen vista of the south polar region and the wildlife that inhabits its chilly landscapes. The opening section, 'Flight Of The Snow Petrel: Glacier Bay', is dedicated to the aviation skills of the genus *pagodroma nivea*. This curious species is one of the most southerly breeding birds, inhabiting the Antarctic mainland and breeding as far south as the south pole itself. A spiralling synth figure fades in at the start of the track. It's soon joined by more scintillating synth sounds that drift along like waves of snowfall. The snow appears to build towards a white-out with the next section, 'Flight Of The Whale-Birds: Blizzard Mountain', where more spiralling synths are joined by a stiff synthesized breeze that pops up unbidden. The layered synths here possibly represent the accumulating layers of snow as we cogitate on the fascinating whale-birds who call the Southern Ocean their home. Due to their saw-like bills, whale-birds are also known as prions (prion being the Greek word for 'saw').

The third section is dedicated to a bird with an image problem, as we encounter 'Flight Of The Albatross: Ice Island'. One of the flying birds with the greatest wingspan (up to 11-and-a-half feet), the albatross became a metaphor for bearing a burden or facing an obstacle, and sailors long believed that killing an albatross brought bad luck. Ant's soundscape here evokes these magnificent birds via more circulating synthesiser and a lightly pattering sequenced synth overlaid by some higher notes. It's all very New Age and ambient, and indeed, this was the album that really opened up that market for Ant. The fourth part, 'White Heaven', displays slow, glacial string synth chords that move like floating ice floes. The suite comes to a close with 'Cathedral Of Ice', which combines a juddering synth matrix with added chords and a few subtle modulations. But it's not all about musical development here; it's more about atmosphere and ambience. An alternate mix of 'Cathedral Of Ice' later appeared on the CD *Private Parts & Extra Pieces*, included with the 2016 Esoteric Records rerelease of *Private Parts & Pieces V-VIII*.

The 'Ice Flight' suite was recorded on a borrowed Roland Jupiter-8 synthesiser, on which Ant went in search of sounds he liked and then recorded them on the spot rather than writing them down. Very much a feature of the album, synthesiser improvisations provided the foundation for many of the tracks on *Slow Waves, Soft Stars*.

'Beachrunner' (Phillips, Berro Garcia)
One of several tracks on the album that were improvised by Ant with guitar buddy Enrique Berro Garcia late one evening in April 1986, 'Beachrunner' features the two guitarists, nicely panned to either side of the stereo picture, as they improvise together over a couple of chords. The acoustic arpeggios double up on occasion, while a classical guitar later moves to some higher picking over chordal strumming. The rapid fade at the end is evidence that this was extracted from a longer improvisation.

'End Of The Affair' (Phillips, Berro Garcia)
Another extract from the 1986 session, the two guitarists on this piece play over a string synth backing track as they build up a romantic ambience. Like most of the tracks on this album, it's a short piece at 2.45, but it makes for a pleasant interlude that contrasts with the many New Age-style synthesized

pieces, giving the album a nice balance. Again, the track fades out rapidly at the end.

'The Golden Pathway' (Phillips)
Even shorter, at 1.39, is 'The Golden Pathway', a piece employed in Ant's soundtrack for Channel 4's 1986 Limehouse production *God's Chosen Car Park*. Shimmering synth chords float across the sound picture, with a sitar-toned synth intermittently rising to the surface. The synth patches provide some interesting choices with varying tones, and the ambience is very New Age in style.

'Behind The Waterfall' (Phillips)
Another New Age-style piece, 'Behind The Waterfall' is notable for Ant's zither contribution among the synthetic waves that wash over the soundscape. A distinctive whistling synth in one speaker draws attention to itself on this side one closer.

'Carnival' (Phillips)
Side two opens with the liveliest track thus far as Ant provides some Martin Carthy-style guitar picking in a partial G tuning. The result is a pure delight. The feel is up-tempo and carnivalesque on this 1.33 workout, supplying a welcome contrast from the ambient drift of much of the material presented on this album.

'Through The Black Hole'/'Pluto Garden' (Phillips)
These two tracks run together and take us in search of those mysterious plugholes of the universe: black holes. The spinning synth that opens this piece imitates the intense gravity well of a black hole, from which no light (or anything else) can hope to escape. Going through these deformations of spacetime would be fraught with peril for the likes of organic creatures like humans, and it's debatable if it would even be possible to do so and survive in any meaningful way. It's still a fascinating exercise to imagine traversing beyond the event horizon of these super-massive objects though, and aided by Ant's music, we can let our imaginations roam free. It's a spaced-out track that boldly goes where no layering of synths has gone before! This intriguing thought experiment finds our black hole warping spacetime in the direction of the outer reaches of our own solar system, emerging in, of all things, a garden on that sadly demoted former planet: the enigmatic Pluto. With a surface temperature of minus 233 degrees Celsius, it's not an ideal place to nurture a garden, it must be said; along with some synth string chords, occasionally prodded by bass synth punctuations, we contemplate this unlikely prospect. Our departure from the very planet where busker Don Partridge claimed to have had his breakfast, according to his 1969 hit single 'Breakfast On Pluto', is accompanied by some percussive

synth notes, which take over in the second half of this engaging space odyssey. An alternate mix of 'Pluto Garden' can be found on the CD *Private Parts & Extra Pieces*, included in the Esoteric Records 2016 rerelease of *Private Parts & Pieces V-VIII*.

'Sospirando' (Phillips)

This gorgeous acoustic guitar composition originated from a demo Ant recorded in the hope of providing the score for the 1983 British drama film *The Honorary Counsel*. Sadly, the film commission went to Stanley Myers in the end. Thankfully, 'Sospirando' found a home on *Slow Waves, Soft Stars* and, for me, it's the highlight of side two. A meditative and quite lovely tune with a pronounced Spanish flavour, it follows a satisfyingly logical structure.

'Elevenses' (Phillips)

Another fascinating, short guitar composition, 'Elevenses' possibly takes its name from the proliferation of 11-beat bars on display here. Ant's fast arpeggio picking accelerates further as the piece progresses, with a few chord strums to close at 3.10.

'Goodbye Serenade' (Phillips)

Written by Ant in 1980, this is an acoustic guitar piece based on slow, downward strums, with a second guitar entering as it proceeds. The melody is gentle and affecting, making for a pleasant 2.29 diversion.

'Bubble And Squeak' (Phillips)

Another piece from 1980, 'Bubble And Squeak' also claims to feature the irrepressible Ralph Bernascone on frying pan! Running at just under one minute, it's a track that certainly doesn't outstay its welcome and proves to be a perky little trifle with a heavily rhythmic feel to the guitar playing, which endears it to the rhythm guitarist in me. There's a nifty little run-up towards the end, providing the fried egg to top our plate of bubble – who can resist a nice bit of bubble and squeak, eh?

'Vanishing Streets'/'Slow Waves, Soft Stars' (Phillips)

The two-part closing track encapsulates the thrust of this album. It runs for a combined duration of 10.31 and is a meditation by Ant on his Casio CZ5000. It's a keyboard he liked for its programmable, overlapping waveforms and envelopes, used to great effect here to evoke a sad, doomy feel in the first half: 'Vanishing Streets'. Another of his improvisations, it's all about atmosphere and ambience as the slowly overlapping synths give way to a deep rush of synth with a touch of reverb. The second half, 'Slow Waves, Soft Stars', is much more restful as we return to the cosmos, the floating waves of sound drifting us gently across the universe with a slow synth pulse intruding like cosmic background radiation, a distant reminder of the dawn of creation in the big bang. No big bangs here, though, just a long, peaceful drift of overlapping synth to close our journey through this seventh edition of the *Private Parts & Pieces* series.

Additional Material
'Jongleur' (Phillips)
Another of Ant's classical guitar workouts, this was recorded following the completion of *Slow Waves, Soft Stars* for a potential new album project. As funding then came through from Amy International for the *Tarka* project, this track remained unreleased until the 2016 Esoteric Records rerelease of *Private Parts & Pieces V-VIII*, when it was included on the fifth CD in the box set, *Private Parts & Extra Pieces II*. Recorded at Englewood Studios in July 1987, 'Jongleur' finds Ant in sprightly mode as fast chordal arpeggios drive the piece forward. It's a graceful sequence with a constant forward momentum. Around the three-minute mark, a triple-time sway prevails, and following a gently shimmering chordal effect, there are a series of liquid runs that point the piece to a conclusion.

'Emerald Forest' (Phillips)
Started at Englewood Studios in March 1983, this spontaneous synth improvisation received some added overdubs at the same studios in January 1987. Opening with whooshing and circulating synth patterns, our magical journey through the 'Emerald Forest' soon brings our first strange encounter, as sporadically recurring percussive-like intrusions shadow our footsteps as we journey onwards. These odd, reverb-treated percussive droplets sound as if something is dropping from the trees to echo on the forest floor, as a long, held synth chord underpins these strange forest noises. It's an atmospherically absorbing listen that would've been right at home on *Slow Waves, Soft Stars*. It's also another track included on the CD *Private Parts & Extra Pieces II*.

'Skylarks Over The Water' (Phillips)
Now, this is lovely. It's another of Ant's classical guitar pieces recorded at Englewood Studios in July 1987. This gorgeously melodic composition transports us to the Scottish Highlands; Ant's Caledonian-flavoured melody effortlessly evokes the title of the piece as we picture said skylarks soaring over a tranquil Scottish loch. Occasional guitar harmonics flicker like sunlight reflected from the water. At 0.55, slow, strummed chording enters the picture, followed by a passage of arpeggio picking and further tempo shifts, as if the wind has whipped up the water of the loch. By the 4.56 point, we return to the beautiful Celtic-tinged melody that started the piece, with a sprinkling of guitar harmonics to close. Again, this was one of the guitar pieces recorded for the project intended to follow *Slow Waves, Soft Stars*, but it didn't see the light of day until added to the *Private Parts & Extra Pieces II* CD much later. It was worth the wait, though.

'Across The Forbidding Horizon' (Phillips)
With its ominous title, you might expect a dark synth improvisation, but instead, we're presented with an interestingly structured 12-string guitar composition. Recorded at Englewood Studios in July 1987, it's another of those guitar pieces originally posited for Ant's next project until *Tarka* took precedence. It's a piece with heaps of atmosphere, starting with guitar notes picking out a melody, followed by three strums per bar, then the same picked melody but this time plucked with two fingers, providing an exotic harmony line to the original melody. This pattern is repeated several times, with small variations creeping in as it develops. The sound of the track is superb, with just the right amount of applied reverb, making it a joy to listen to. Around 1.12, things move into a cyclic, picked pattern implying a drone effect, as in Indian music. Atmospherically, there is a slightly forbidding feel to the piece as it progresses, but it remains a fascinating listening experience. Like many of these additional tracks, it was made available on the *Private Parts & Extra Pieces II* CD.

'End Of The Affair II' (Phillips, Berro Garcia)
This second revisitation to the termination of said affair is a further excerpt from the spring 1986 Phillips/Berro Garcia sessions, probably from the same long ramble the duo took a snippet from for the *Slow Waves, Soft Stars* album. It's backed by a constant synth chord as the two guitarists improvise over it with some impressive spontaneous interplay, showing what talented musicians they are. In places, the synth sounds move from a gargling effect to ethereal choral patches, and the tone of the music remains sorrowful, as you would imagine at the end of an affair. It's quite a hypnotic track, and there's some acoustic guitar hammering in the fade.

'Beachrunner II' (Phillips, Berro Garcia)
From the same spring 1986 sessions comes this second excerpt from 'Beachrunner', a snippet of which previously featured on *Slow Waves, Soft Stars*. This second slice, like the first, moves calmly over a couple of chords as Ant and his Argentinian pal Enrique Berro Garcia – panned to either side of the stereo picture – swap licks, chords and arpeggios from their arsenal of techniques, and the result is an extremely relaxed improvisation. As the excerpt closes, there are some flickering guitar harmonics.

'Unheard Cry' (guitar demo) (Phillips)
This is the earliest demo of what would become a song and feature on Ant's 1992 album *Private Parts & Pieces VIII: New England*. Here, it's just a guitar demo, which was recorded at Englewood Studios in July 1987. It's performed on 12-string guitar and the verse parts bear a strong relationship to an earlier song, the marvellous 'Sistine'. There is a contrasting second section and a nice middle passage. It would, however, find its perfect form, once furnished with lyrics, to provide another valued contribution to Ant's canon of songs.

'A Place To Rest' (Phillips)

Another of the 12-string pieces recorded at Englewood Studios in July 1987, 'A Place To Rest' is of interest for its unusual time signature of 10/8. This gives it a singular forward motion as the chiming 12-string negotiates another of Ant's logical sequences. Despite its irregular motion, it does remain a restful piece, as the title reflects.

'The Riddle Of The Sands' (Phillips)

Taking its title from the popular 1903 Erskine Childers espionage novel of the same name, 'The Riddle Of The Sands' was another candidate for the aborted follow-up to *Slow Waves, Soft Stars*. It was recorded in July 1987 at Englewood Studios and is a substantial beast, with a duration of over ten minutes. It's another of Ant's classical guitar pieces, and the opening passage consists of downward-moving guitar figures with a twisty, winding feel, moving to a higher octave. The pace remains relaxed with the merest hint of Eastern overtones amid the classicism. Some arpeggio picking traverses a delicious sequence reflecting Ant's supreme structural logic. As it moves to some higher picking, there's a possibly unconscious nod to the mode employed by The Rolling Stones on the number-one 1966 hit single 'Paint It Black' (a reminder of The Anon's musical preferences all those years ago!).

Around 4.35, the pace picks up for a passage of faster picking, evoking a spinning effect. As the music moves between two chords, there's a touch of Flamenco styling on show, along with a coruscating shimmer that Ant coaxes from his guitar. Perhaps this passage reflects the treacherous sands described in Childers' book, as you can imagine the yachtsman protagonist of that novel navigating channels through the shifting mudflats with nautical skill. It's also a piece that would lend itself to orchestration, such is its sturdy structure.

Around the seven-minute mark, there's a recapitulation of the opening sequence of the piece, and it then moves up the fretboard for some picking, hammering, and short, mazy runs before terminating at 10.18. It's the final track on *Private Parts & Extra Pieces II*.

Tarka (1988)

Anthony Phillips: acoustic guitars, keyboards
Harry Williamson: acoustic guitars, keyboards
Krysia Osostowicz: violin
Ann Morfee: violin
Janet Crouch: cello
Anne Glover: oboe
Ian Hardwick: oboe
Lindsay Cooper: bassoon
Nick Cox: clarinet, bass clarinet
Andrew Anscombe: French horn
Didier Malherbe: flute, piccolo, soprano saxophone
Julie Allis: harp
Guy Evans: percussion
Dave Sawyer: percussion
The National Philharmonic Orchestra, conducted by Jeremy Gilbert
Recorded: CTS Studios, Wembley, by John Richards; Gooseberry Studios, Tulse Hill, by John Gibbons, assisted by David Robertson-Campbell; additional recording at Vic's Place, Clapham, London; digital editing and mastering by Mike Ross and CBS Studios, London
Producer: Simon Heyworth
Record label: PRT
Released: 31 October 1988, PRT; CD rerelease, Blueprint, June 1996

Back in 1975-76, Ant had been doing some recording with Harry Williamson (see chapter on *Private Parts & Pieces*), and around this time, the pair collaborated on a project with film director David Cobham – with the blessing of Harry Williamson's father and *Tarka The Otter* author Henry Williamson – to provide a suitable soundtrack for Cobham's planned film adaption of the book. Sadly, by the time of the film's release in 1979, it had been decided that the Phillips/Williamson music would not now be employed for the soundtrack, and Cobham instead commissioned Devonian ethnomusicologist David Fanshawe to compose the film's soundtrack.

The Phillips/Williamson music, therefore, sat in limbo for another 11 years until, in 1987, Amy International stumped up an advance to complete the recording of *Tarka*. For this purpose, Ant hired a Fostex 16-track tape recorder for use in his own studio, now known as Vic's Place.

Also available during this era was a limited-edition cassette release on Voiceprint Records boss Rob Ayling's Ottersongs imprint, entitled *Tarka Music*. Side one consisted of Ant and Harry on guitars and keyboards performing themes from *Tarka*, while on side two, the pair were joined by the London Philharmonic Orchestra. The third variation of this music finally appeared in 2024 on the CD *Gypsy Suite*, which featured the original *Tarka* demos from 1975-1976.

With its convoluted history, it was quite an achievement for Ant and Harry when the *Tarka* CD was released on PRT on 31 October 1988. It proved to be a fine work that exceeded its original conception as soundtrack music and, with its strong symphonic structure, can justifiably be regarded as a long-form work of real substance. *Tarka* received its live debut in February 2010 when an Australian symphony orchestra performed the work in Melbourne to great acclaim.

The original artwork for *Tarka* was provided by Main Artery and consisted of a scenic photograph by Steve Speller of actress Susan George surrounded by a misty halo with a gothic-looking tower in the background. This photo was spread over both sides of the cover, with the rear view of foliage only. When Blueprint reissued the album on CD, it was replaced by a more suitable photo of an otter swimming in a stream, which was credited to Nico G.

'Movement I' (Williamson, Phillips)
The co-written opening movement begins with a scene-setting evocation of the book's opening chapter: 'The First Year'. The duo's twin acoustics strum gently across the opening chords, and Simon Heyworth's crystal-clear production is instantly evident in the gorgeously subtle reverb reflections applied to the guitars and shimmering string chords, bringing the Devonian riverscape of Owlery Holt to life before our ears. After 37 seconds, the guitars take over with arpeggios and runs that outline several of the themes to be developed as the piece progresses. Some rhythmic picking and guitar harmonics introduce a passage with an odd, clipped time signature and this theme is picked up by the flute of Didier Malherbe (ex-Gong), combining sweetly with a reflective oboe line.

The next few passages are subtitled 'Weare Water' and 'The Golden Pool', and here, the woodwind section perfectly conjure the feel of bubbling water. At 4.25, a sweet solo violin takes over, joined by a complementary oboe. A more playful passage of flute, oboe and celeste represents the section subtitled 'Moon Play', where it's easy to imagine otters at play at night under a full moon.

At 7.00, piano arpeggios underpin a passage where a memorable initial theme returns. Over the next few minutes, a clipped time signature introduces the woodwind section, who again work their magic to evoke 'Corncrake Meadow' – the bassoon of Lindsay Cooper (ex-Henry Cow) being particularly noticeable. With an underlying, circulating riff, the sound here is almost oriental in feel. The tender oboe theme from 'Corncrake Meadow' would later provide one of the themes for the album's closing track: 'The Anthem'. The ninth minute brings a crossfade into the final section, 'Root Walk', in which the picked guitar figures of the early part of the movement return to point it to a conclusion. A dancing theme played by the orchestra circulates round as the first movement fades out at 11.24.

'Movement II' (Williamson)

The second movement represents the 'River And Estuary' chapter of the book and is a Harry Williamson composition. The first part is subtitled 'Moonfield' and it opens with rising string chords that slowly emerge, sounding like a more clement variation on the opening Mellotron chords of Genesis' 'Watcher Of The Skies'. Around 0.58, a flute figure drifts into some variations from the assembled woodwind section and there's nice modulation at 1.49 that soon morphs into some speedy guitar arpeggios with an early Genesis flavour. At 3.09, a new theme introduces 'Waymoor', with its rising feel peppered with some tidily arranged string glissandi. This section displays a subdued magnificence, and its themes are logically developed and expanded with some sitar-like twangs embedded into the mix.

As we move into 'The Estuary', at 5.16, a flute sails high above the strings, evoking the flight of birds over the river mouth. Then, unexpectedly, at 6.19, we move into a percussive section, the first major change from the symphonic feel of the piece so far. This initiates the 'Salmon Hunt' as the ensemble's two percussionists, Guy Evans and Dave Sawyer, go to town on this percussion-heavy passage, along with strumming, rhythmic guitars and an engaging brass line that sounds like a trumpet. The percussive section is reminiscent of that on Mike Oldfield's classic 1975 album *Ommadawn*, as the bongos roll and Didier Malherbe takes centre stage with a free-flowing solo on soprano saxophone that is positively jazzy in its capricious, free movement. It's a marvellous interlude.

At 8.30, the 'Moonfield' theme that opened the movement returns with those pensive, rising string chords. This builds into some arpeggio guitar picking as the orchestra build on the themes, underpinned by celli moving in a regular pattern beneath. The penultimate section of the movement is titled 'The Burrows', and in this mainly orchestral passage, there are some atmospheric ambient noises, perhaps representing the squeaks and squeals of the otters. The music here has a grandiose sweep that is elating. The final section of the second movement progresses to a very Holst-like climax, especially the swelling brass section underlying the strings, after which the movement closes with some tuned percussion taking up the theme to conclude this final section, subtitled 'Bag Leap', at 15.43. On the Blueprint CD rerelease, some additional music was added in the form of 'The Rising Spring', bringing the running time up to 16.20.

'Movement III' (Phillips)

The third movement represents 'The Hunt' and commences with some floating orchestral chords, aptly subtitled 'The Foreboding'. By the second minute, the music bubbles up with piano underpinning it. Some choppy celli and timpani find this movement embarking on a more dramatic thrust as the music rises and falls like surging water. Our musical journey takes us into 'Dark Hams Wood' and on to the 'Pool Of Six Herons', combining woodwind and celeste in a circulating theme. At 4.30, tubular bells chime over whirlpool-like keyboards, and by 5.26, the music starts to become more strident, with marching celli evoking a sense of impending danger, reflecting the subtitle 'Escape To The Estuary'. The orchestral sweep of the music rises to a crescendo of crashing waves, which then falls to a slower tempo before a resurgence that conjures the vision of thrashing otters in troubled waters. Some earlier themes are recapitulated before developing into a fast triplet climax at 10.00. The subtitle of this section is 'Beam Weir'.

A passage of gentle arpeggio harp reflects the arrival at 'The Kelp Pool', falling into another dramatic section of agitation from the orchestra, complete with crashing cymbals. Following on from 'The Island Run', the orchestra finally descend to calmer waters. The closing sequence is subtitled 'Ebb Tide' and has a gentler feel, again reminiscent of Gustav Holst but this time in more reflective mode. Sad minor chords enter the picture in the 12th minute as the music slowly rises and falls, moving to tinkling celeste to conclude the third movement at 15.23.

'The Anthem' (Phillips, Heyworth)

Released as a CD single in slightly edited form in 1988 and titled 'The Anthem From Tarka', this end piece plays off two memorable themes from the album over a programmed drum box of bass drum and 'stick'. The oboe is most prominent over the dead-slow triple-time metre. It's kept simple and melodic, with the woodwind backed by floating string chords. The effect is rather charming, as the two melodic themes are rich and tuneful. There's no real development over its 4.41 duration, but it's still a very pleasant listen, although, sadly, it never got anywhere near the singles chart at the time. The CD single also features the then-non-album track 'The Rising Spring' and short excerpts from the first and third movements of 'Tarka', plus the extended 6.05 album version of 'The Anthem'. As well as being the single from the album, 'The Anthem' also makes for a nice capstone to the entrancing musical journey enacted through the *Tarka* album.

Missing Links Volume 1: Finger Painting (1989)

Personnel:
Anthony Phillips: keyboards, guitars
The Gabrieli String Quartet, conducted by Jeremy Gilbert ('Boulevard Of Fallen Leaves')
Producer: Anthony Phillips, assisted by Rog Patterson
Record label: Occasional
Released: December 1989, Occasional; CD rerelease, Brainworks, 1992; CD rerelease, Blueprint, 1996; CD rerelease with The Sky Road and Time & Tide, Voiceprint, January 2011; CD rerelease as part of Missing Links I-IV, Esoteric, November 2020

This was the first release in Ant's *Missing Links* series, collating examples of his library music through the years. This first volume is subtitled *A Collection Of Television And Library Music 1979 – 89* and provides an interesting sidelight to his main sequence releases and the *Private Parts & Pieces* series. It was originally released in December 1989 as a private cassette on Ant's own Occasional imprint in a limited edition of 1,000 copies.

'Force Majeure' (Phillips)

Kicking off what Ant refers to as the album's 'First XI' (another cricketing reference!) is this short slab of library music, drawn from the vaults of the Atmosphere music library and recorded in 1987. Circulating programmed synthesiser spins in a fast rhythmic coil while punctuating bass-end synth notes stab. The drama increases as the stabbing notes get more pronounced, and a synth melody rises above the more rhythmic elements. The title translates to English as 'major force' and refers to the event of exceptional circumstances nullifying the terms of a contract.

'Mountain Voices' (Phillips)

Another short piece recorded in 1987, 'Mountain Voices' opens with a low drone note as an oscillating synth washes over the landscape. It's all rather ambient as drifting synth strings sail above the oscillations as the track proceeds.

'Lord Of The Smoking Mirror' (Phillips)

Reflecting the piece's dramatic title, deep, stalking bass notes on synthesiser are punctuated by staccato stabbing. There are some effective reverb reflections that carry to one side of the stereo mix, creating the illusion of cavernous space – perhaps representing the lair of the smoke-wreathed Lord in question. The piece does have a rather abrupt ending at 2.57.

'Sea Horses' (Phillips)

This short piece does aptly reflect its title, as sequenced bubbling synthesisers with rising string chords perfectly evoke those fascinating creatures of the ocean.

'Dungeons' (Phillips)

Another short, atmospheric composition that, like many in this collection, is built on a foundation of synthesisers. The somewhat doom-laden synth punctuations conjure the gloom of a dark, dank dungeon on a piece that would perhaps suit a historical documentary on the darker side of medieval existence.

Amongst the shadowy synths, the distant sound of a circulating sequencer is detectable over to one side of the stereo mix, while, down in the stygian depths, all hope appears to be fading fast.

'Between The Rings' (Phillips)

Recorded in 1983, this track would be an ideal short piece of music for an astronomical documentary on the glorious rings of Saturn. A cascading synth sequence, which vacillates between tones, could perhaps represent the tiny moonlets that stream between the broad rings of Saturn in the so-called Cassini Division, which appears to Earth-based telescopes as a dark gap in the plane of the rings.

'Evening Ascent' (Phillips)

While we're talking of space, this is another track with a distinct spacey feel to it. Mellow tones resembling an electric piano are joined by a lightly whooshing sound, but the most effective feature of this track, which was recorded in 1983, are the synth glissandi that ascend as string chords build around them. It's an addictive effect as the ever-ascending synth notes curve upwards.

'Streamer' (Phillips)

The speedy synth sequencing on this 1983 track is almost dizzying in its relentless spin. It appears to be shooting sparks off the main sequence as it progresses. Short but dynamic, the track peters out at only 1.14.

'After The Rain' (Phillips)

The sound here feels like it has a guitar mixed in somewhere, although I guess it could be a sample. The phrases have rest bars between them and there is also an element of percussion in the mix. Some staccato punctuation is introduced, along with some softer electric piano tones and more guitar-like sounds.

'Rottweiler' (Phillips)

Deep synth notes on a crotchet beat give this 1983 track a relentless forward drive. More circulating sequenced synth is in evidence, along with a degree of whooshing. I'm not certain of the intended purpose of this sample piece from the Atmosphere library, but I would say it doesn't quite live up to the image of the dog it's named after!

'Sad Fish' (Phillips)

Closing the 'First XI' is this piece, recorded in 1983, an instrumental ode to a depressed denizen of the deep. It's a reflective affair, with synth notes bathed in reverb as they move up then down. Some tinkling synth conjures up tiny bubbles rising to the surface of the water while lighter synth chords drift like seaweed above.

'A Song' (Phillips)

Opening the 'Second XI' is this 36-second tune, which would indeed provide a fine melody for a song. Here, it sports a brief but pretty guitar melody supported by some string chords. It was recorded in 1979 and has an obvious connection to 'And A Prayer', another short snippet that appears later during this side of the album.

'God's Chosen Car Park Suite' (Phillips)

A suite in three parts, this was written for the Limehouse Production, Channel 4 TV drama of the same name. The programme was broadcast on 1 December 1986 and starred actors Ian Lavender, John Bird and Peter Capaldi. Ant provided the music for this dramatic epic about a new Messiah appearing in an underground car park. The suite opens with 'Processional', where some clattering percussion samples, with repeat echo reverb, introduce some synthetic strings.

The second part, 'Meditation', has a lighter synth touch and is vaguely electro-pop in feel. A deep, dark whooshing sound introduces the final sequence, 'Cave Painting', with its combination of string chords and darker synth notes anticipating a slowly creeping ominous feel. I guess it's commissions like this that enabled Ant to stock his fridge and feed the cat around this time.

'Tropical Moon Over Dorking Suite' (Phillips)

Another Limehouse Production drama for Channel 4, *Tropical Moon Over Dorking* starred Pauline Collins and Michael Gambon and was broadcast on 31 March 1985, repeated on 13 December 1986, making the latter a good month for Ant, with two productions airing that featured his soundtrack. We earlier encountered one piece from this drama ('Erotic Strings'), as it was on both the compilation album *Harvest Of The Heart* (1985) and the 1991 reissue CD of *A Catch At The Tables*. Here, we are presented with three more, the first of which is subtitled 'Estrangement'. It introduces a sense of sweeping romance with its big piano chords and Parisian ambience via a piping synth melody line. The romantic feel continues with the second selection, 'Myra's Dream', where the reflective melody is awash in synth string chords and sweeping triple-time piano. It closes with 'Reconciliation' via some very high dancing synth notes and a melodic string-washed denouement.

Anthony Phillips 1977-1990 ... *On Track*

'Fountain Pool' (Phillips)
This 29-second trifle from 1986 functioned as the soundtrack to a New Zealand lamb TV commercial, to which Ant added the word '*Shame!*' in his sleeve notes. Some slightly wobbly, treated synth patches compete with a rippling synth undertow to complete Ant's brief for the commercial.

'C.Q.' (Phillips)
Recorded in 1984, this 1.01 snippet was also the title of another Limehouse production for Channel 4 that was first aired on 11 October 1984, with a repeat on 6 December 1986, adding a third royalty bonus to Ant's income for that month! This drama saw a radio ham linking up with a round-the-world yachtsman with life-changing consequences. The very high synth line plays a melody with a somewhat disconcerting feel; the purposeful off-key movement at points evokes uncertainty. It moves to a highly whimsical final chord.

'Three Piece Suite' (Phillips)
Recorded in 1984, this triptych was employed as an audio-visual for National Panasonic. The three short sections are subtitled 'To The Shrine', 'Through The Forest' and 'Towards The Light'. It's based around a drum box rhythm on a tom-tom setting with various sequenced synth lines running through it. The sound has a very 1980s vibe, and the last section has an identical sonic quality to the sound of the album *1984*.

'Boulevard Of Fallen Leaves' (Phillips)
This track comes across as refreshing, surrounded as it is by more synthesized fare. Here, the Gabrieli String Quartet, conducted by Jeremy Gilbert, perform a lovely triple-time arrangement with a big, romantic swell. It moves to common time for a passage that sounds as if various woodwind instruments have also been employed, although none are credited, leading to the assumption these could be keyboard samples. To close, we return to the fetching triple-time string arrangement that sweeps beautifully to close a track that provides a delicious sonic treat for the ears.

'Land Of The Dragons Suite' (Phillips)
The soundtrack to a 1989 Anglia TV documentary about wildlife in Hong Kong, this suite is another highlight of the album with its distinctive oriental feel. It opens with the main 'Land Of The Dragons' theme underpinned by a deep-toned synth note. There are some excellent samples used here that are evocative of the Far East destination featured in the documentary. Especially noteworthy are the breathy, pipe-like samples and the equally effective koto-like plucked samples that place us right in the Orient. The music uses dynamics effectively, where soft/loud contrasts abound as we move through the subtitled sections: 'Kites' and 'Harbour At Sunset'. 'The Dance Of The Crabs' is a very visually descriptive passage as a fast, sequenced section of

tuned percussion is accompanied by drumbeats and underpinned by bass synth moves. There are some koto-like pings as we contemplate the terpsichorean skills of the crustaceans involved.

The fifth section sees our crabby friends meeting up with a sand octopus as breathy synth samples sustain a note, a vibraphone sound meets up with a disembodied choral effect and a celeste plays an oriental melody. An authentic violin sample then takes over the main melody, leading us to the sixth part, where we cogitate on the question: 'Do The Shrimps Know They're Chinese?' – the jury's out on that one, I think! Great title, though. During this section, things become more crepuscular until a bold return to the opening 'Land Of The Dragons' theme sews it all up in great style.

'And A Prayer' (Phillips)

This 1.08 snippet reprises the musical ideas in 'A Song' that opened the 'Second XI', this time with sweeping string chords underlining what a lovely little melodic idea this is.

'Tierra Del Fuego' (Phillips)

We head towards Cape Horn on the southern tip of South America with this short musical sketch of strummed chords and a high synth melody that moves higher towards the conclusion of the piece.

'Paradise Found' (Phillips)

With its gentle piano arpeggios and overlying melody, this piece refers not to poet John Milton but to skincare in the form of the soundtrack to a 1979 TV commercial for Oil of Ulay (later to become 'Olay'). The second half of this 2.07 piece bears a startling similarity to the reversed chord sounds employed on 'Wind-Tales', the track that opened Ant's first solo album, *The Geese & The Ghost*.

Slow Dance (1990)

Personnel:

Anthony Phillips: Emax I, Jupiter 8, Casio CZ 5000, Roland 808, Tom drum machine, Alvarez 12-string guitar, Fender Stratocaster electric guitar, Yari classical guitar, Ovation six-string guitar, Gretsch fretless bass, Yamaha QX5 sequencer (Part 2 only)

Martin Robertson: clarinet
Ian Hardwick: oboe
Michael Cox: flute, piccolo
Torbjorn Hultmark: trumpet
Julie Allis: harp
Ian Thomas: drums
Frank Ricotti: percussion
John Owen Edwards: conductor
Recorded: Vic's Place, June 1988 – March 1989
Produced and engineered by Anthony Phillips and Simon Heyworth
Additional engineering by John Gibbons
Remastered by Simon Heyworth at Super Audio Mastering, Chagford, Devon
Artwork: Steve Murray and associates
Record label: Virgin
Released: 24 September 1990, Virgin; CD rerelease, Blueprint, 1995; CD rerelease three-disc edition, Esoteric, June 2017; CD rerelease, two-disc edition, Esoteric, April 2024

Following the *Tarka* sessions of 1988, Ant began to consider another long-form composition with a possible appeal to the burgeoning New Age market. Following Brian Eno's pioneering promotion of the joys of ambient music in the late 1970s, the New Age tag became attached to this genre in the 1980s, and it began to claim a bigger slice of the market, especially with the advent of the compact disc. The ambient bias of Ant's *Slow Waves, Soft Stars* had appealed greatly to New Age music fans, and he had also become involved with New Age musician Denis Quinn, for whom he produced the albums *Open Secret* in 1987 and *Mystic Heart* in 1989. Ant's US record label, Passport, had promised him an advance, encouraging his management company, Hit & Run, to offer him a loan to update his recording gear. Thus, Ant felt prepared to attempt an ambitious long-form composition for his next main sequence album. Inspired, he was able to work quickly on new ideas that he could combine to create a large-scale, grandiose piece of music – which would eventually coalesce into *Slow Dance*. Unfortunately for Ant, Passport Records ceased trading in 1989, so his promised advance failed to materialise, putting him under financial pressure and in dire need of a reliable outlet for his new project, which, by now, had been given the working title *Album '88*. In cahoots with Simon Heyworth, Ant lashed together two 16-track tape recorders to give more options as the recording became more complex. Although monitoring the two machines was challenging, in the long run, it aided the clarity of production on what was fast becoming Ant's *magnum opus*.

Financially, the cavalry came over the hill in the shape of a contract with Virgin Records, who liked what they heard and signed Ant up for his new project. A fortuitous by-product of this was an offer from Virgin to engage in a series of CD rereleases of his back catalogue with additional bonus tracks, especially appreciated by his fanbase at the time. *Slow Dance* would prove to be a fan favourite and it's also a favourite of Ant himself. It's an album of timeless appeal that raised Ant's profile for the new decade as the 1990s beckoned.

The album artwork was, this time, provided by Steve Murray and associates, and evinced a New Age vibe with its moody shades of green and impressions of leaf motifs set within it. It wasn't quite Peter Cross territory, but its understated ambience captured the spirit of the (new) age.

'Slow Dance (Part 1)' (Phillips)

The third of Ant's long-form works, *Slow Dance* was very much a refinement of the style previously established with *1984* and *Tarka*, combining the best aspects of these differing approaches. The synth-based, technological style of the former and the orchestral, symphonic style of the latter came together in a perfect blend within *Slow Dance*. This is not to say it's working the same musical themes as those albums, but tonally, it feels like a definite development of the two approaches of these earlier albums. The work is divided into two parts, one for each side of the vinyl album. 'Slow Dance (Part 1)' opens with the underlying chords of its beautiful initial theme, to which it will return in various guises throughout the work. These chords have an organ-like quality, courtesy of one of Ant's trio of synthesisers he employed on this project. Behind this uplifting opening chord sequence runs an unusual-sounding electronic tone. It's a similar (but not identical) sound to that employed on side two of David Bowie's 1977 album *"Heroes"*, running intermittently through the side two instrumental 'Moss Garden' (check it out!). It's certainly a peculiar and disturbing sound that, for some reason, I equate to resembling a sonic representation of a rupture in the space/time continuum as, to my ears, it sounds like a slow sonic ripping behind the majestic opening synth chords. However, as the orchestration swells and the melodic theme sails atop the glorious backing chords, we soon find ourselves contemplating the neo-classical grace of this gorgeous initial theme. Contrast is provided via two acoustic guitars lending a Celtic flavour to the music and again bringing Mike Oldfield to mind. A modulation at 2.48 darkens the tone a degree, but light soon returns with a lightly piping variation on the theme.

The first major change from the initial set of variations occurs after five minutes, as a marimba-like figure begins to sound more playful, and with the woodwind variations overlaying it, recalls the biblical Salome and 'The Dance Of The Seven Veils'. I would say there's also a definite nod to the feel of

Nikolai Rimsky-Korsakov's 1888 symphonic suite *Scheherazade*. It's a beautifully worked passage that moves in conjunction with the sweeping orchestral theme playing off against it. At 9.39, there's a delightful on-beat pulse, with a flute-like tone and a light and airy movement evoking the slowly beating wings of a graceful swan in flight.

A major change in mood occurs after 12 minutes with a heavy percussive passage of click-clacking drums, along with a deeper thudding. This soon doubles the beat as tuned percussion plays atop this hammering mayhem. Each section modulates up a tone in a stepped motion that raises the listener higher and higher. Some electric guitar notes are introduced along with this rhythm in an excitedly energised section that, after several minutes, collapses back to the earlier theme but this time with a variation of a synth chorale, moving into a grand build-up with timpani and organ-like chords.

At 15.29, gentle tuned percussion introduces a guitar adagio, with Ant's tuneful, layered electric guitars in a matrix of harmony. Some nice, gentle dynamic shifts in this section overlay piping melodic themes, contrasting with tinkling celeste sounds and Julie Allis' plucked harp. It's a section with a strong folk flavour, juxtaposing with the neo-classical sections that return to fabulous effect. The final three minutes of 'Slow Dance (Part 1)' build on the guitar adagio section with its gentle jog-along rhythm with a drum beat on the third beat in every bar. Ant's very civilized-sounding guitar licks become more emotive until the brief return of the synth chorale, leading to an unexpectedly playful ending at 24 minutes – a deliciously whimsical twist on which to end part one!

'Slow Dance (Part 2)' (Phillips)

Part two fades in with a gently tumbling, cyclic, repeated marimba-toned riff sporting an irregular feel. It's underpinned by slowly pulsing percussion with occasional bass-end synth intrusions. The effect is rather hypnotic and eases us gently into the second half of the piece. After a few minutes, this introductory passage is replaced by a solo synth melody, as floating string chords provide a perfect cushion underneath. At 3.56, a beautiful synth melody is supported by a sympathetic woodwind arrangement until, at 4.18, a pulsing bass note, playing on the beat, heralds the entrance of marimba tones, replete with repeat echoes that open up space in the music to let it breathe. Some subtle guitar arpeggios add to the sense of slow build in this reflective passage as it moves forward on floating string chords. The woodwind department expand on the beautiful melody that appeared earlier. As the next section builds, based on a lightly pattering drum box rhythm, a rather cute melody enters the fray, and Ant plays some nice fretless bass as his bass lines slide under the unfolding themes of this balletic composition. Interestingly, the album gained its title of *Slow Dance* after a comment by Declan Colgan at Virgin Records, as the music suggested to him the movement of ballet. Ant went for this suggestion, perhaps imagining the elusive ballerina Lucy dancing to its beautiful themes. Whatever, it was certainly a more suitable title than the previous two working titles: *Album '88* and *Project 2*.

Next, a sequencer is employed to provide a cyclic synth figure over which a playful piccolo dances. The music moves through several modulations as the magnificent initial theme, first heard in part one, is brought back in and developed in tandem with the thematic progressions introduced in part two until, at 12.00, a juddering synth chord breaks the spell. This prefaces an oceanic build of resonant cello and string chords that climaxes in part two's most exciting section.

This commences at 14.18 with a bedding of sequenced synth, combined with a pattering drum box rhythm, overlaid with big, orchestral chords and speedy figures played by chopping violins. The urgent drive of this section is positively thrilling – it's a four-minute sequence known unofficially as 'No Way Out', and on the Esoteric CD rereleases, the extra disc entitled *Slow Dance Vignettes* features both an alternate mix of this section and another mix featuring drummer Ian Thomas. The short, sharp phrases of the choppy violin in this section magnify the exhilaration of this passage, as a series of trumpet fanfares over the skittering drum box rhythm move the delirium to another level. It makes for an enthralling ride. Some guitar interjections precede a slower top-line synth melody over the careering rhythm with impressive thematic development that unites the themes of the whole work in an organically complete way. At 18.34, the 'No Way Out' section comes to an end. The passage that follows it places one of its themes in a new context, as high synth notes play over a drum box downbeat every two bars. String chords then drift in for a further floating interlude, with suggestions of previous themes appearing as the music slowly modulates upwards, intensifying in grandiosity.

The closing section of part two returns to its opening sequence, reoccurring at 22.29 with a cyclic, repeating movement in an elusive time signature. It's a peaceful postlude to a marvellous work, certainly one of Ant's best efforts. As the marimba-like tones and bell-like tinkles cycle around this sequence, a feeling of tranquillity descends. A lovely choral sample floats by in the background among the gently tinkling bells, invoking a truly mesmerising ambience to close *Slow Dance* in perfect peace. It completes one of Ant's most hauntingly beautiful creations and is a complete artistic triumph. It's an album with great appeal to progressive rock fans, classical music lovers, New Age aficionados and all those who appreciate beautiful melodies, harmonic invention and musical adventure in general.

Additional Material
'Themes From Slow Dance' (Phillips)
This mix, allowing the orchestral string parts of the work to be heard in isolation, was recorded at CBS Studios in February 1989. It really brings out

the inherent beauty of the orchestral parts on this album. All the recordings below were additional tracks appended to the Esoteric CD rereleases of *Slow Dance*.

'No Way Out' (alternate mix) (Phillips)

This alternate mix allows elements of the acoustic guitar and percussion to be appreciated alongside the string parts.

'A Slower Dance' (Phillips)

This shorter piece, highlighting themes from the album, was recorded as a potential single at the time. It incorporates part of another piano piece Ant was working on at the time.

'Guitar Adagio From Slow Dance' (Phillips)

Another mix of the guitar adagio section from side one, it highlights Ant's gorgeous guitar parts for this section.

'Touch Me Deeply' (demo) (Phillips)

Recorded in the autumn of 1988 at Vic's Place, 'Touch Me Deeply' was a potential song that Ant wrote a few years earlier. You can certainly hear the possibilities inherent in this medium-tempo demo of a song-like chord sequence based on a matrix of what sounds like electric piano with punctuating bass guitar lines and some synth string pads. Although sounding somewhat incomplete, it's still a tidy little sequence and you can easily imagine its title words fitting perfectly with what sounds like a possible chorus section.

'Clarinet Sleigh Ride' (Phillips)

This seasonal-sounding clarinet tune has a triple-time, sequenced synth backing that circulates around in the background while the catchy clarinet line tootles happily above. It's contrasted by some descending chords on synth that positively yell 'Christmas' at you. With a few sleigh bells added, it would be easy to imagine this cheery trifle as an instrumental Yuletide single in the same mode as Mike Oldfield's 1975 hit single 'In Dulci Jubilo'. A missed opportunity that might have been worth a shot.

'Slow Dance Single Demo' (Phillips)

First released on the 1998 CD *The Archive Collection Volume One*, this is another attempt by Ant to distil the themes from *Slow Dance* into a single format. Recorded in the spring of 1990 at Vic's Place, with a working title of 'Soft Single', Virgin Records failed to detect commercial potential in it at the time, so it waited until 1998 to see the light of day, then appeared again on the Esoteric CD rereleases of *Slow Dance* in 2017 and 2024. It cleverly distils several of the wonderful melodies from 'Slow Dance' into a catchier prospect, backed by a slowly sauntering drum box with guitar arpeggios and a central melodic line.

'No Way Out' (original mix with drums) (Phillips)
As previously mentioned, this additional mix of 'No Way Out' had the added drums of Ian Thomas, as it was thought that this section would benefit from real drums. The eventual realisation was that the passage worked better with just the drum machine. A welcome addition to the bonus tracks on the Esoteric CD reissues, it's still a supremely exciting piece of music.

'Lenta Chorum' (Phillips)
The penultimate section of Part 2, this is the strings-only version of this passage and glorious it is, too, making another welcome bonus track for the Esoteric CD rereleases of *Slow Dance*.

Archive Collection Volume I

The next three chapters cover archive material from the pre-1990 period that was later made available via the compilations *Archive Collection Volume I* and *Archive Collection Volume II*. The first of these CD sets was released by Blueprint Records in 1998, with the second collection following in 2004. These releases were superseded in 2022 when Esoteric Records released the five-CD box set *Archive Collection Volume I & Volume II*. Not only did this cover the previously released archive material, but it also saw the long-delayed release of music from Ant's *Masquerade* project, recorded in conjunction with Richard Scott between 1980 and 1983. So, here we'll look at all these additional recordings as presented on the five-CD Esoteric Records box set.

'Back To Pluto' (Phillips)
Fading in with a generated tone which grows louder as it moves to ascend into a big Mellotron string chord, this synth doodle, recorded at Vic's Place in March 1987, is a previously unreleased recording from the sessions for *Slow Waves, Soft Stars*. It returns us once again to that enigmatic world on the edge of our Solar System, first discovered by American astronomer Clyde Tombaugh in 1930. According to the sleeve notes, another apparent highlight of this track is that it features 'Ralph Bernascone on meteorite'!

'Promenade' (Phillips)
Recorded in the winter of 1986 at Vic's Place, this is an alternate version of a track that was later rerecorded for *Private Parts & Pieces IX: Dragonfly Dreams*. Here, Ant plays a heavily flanged 12-string as he picks arpeggios while a faint keyboard pad underpins in the background. The piece has a contemplative drift and is quite atmospheric.

'Take This Heart' (Phillips, Rutherford)
This recording is a summer 1972 Send Barns demo of the modern hymn Ant composed with his long-time writing partner, Mike Rutherford. It features Ant on what sounds like an old upright piano. His left-hand chords are decorated with some spreading right-hand chords at the higher end of the keyboard in this engaging sequence. Towards the end of the track, there are a series of rising runs followed by a descending glissando. Also notable are the nifty triplet underpins with his left hand beneath the right-hand action. The song was eventually recorded by the Charterhouse Choral Society in October 1973 and released by Charisma Records on the various artists album *Beyond An Empty Dream* in April 1975.

'Beside The Water's Edge' (Phillips, Rutherford)
This demo from the summer of 1977 revives another of the songs written with Mike Rutherford in the very productive early-Genesis era of 1969. Ant

strums on his 12-string guitar while singing the vocal. It's a recording of demo quality and rather low fidelity, but the pretty melody comes through loud and clear via Ant's charming vocal performance. There's some rhythmic 12-string chording providing contrast halfway through the song, and this returns after a further verse as the song draws to a close.

'The Geese & The Ghost' (kiddies mix) (Phillips, Rutherford)
The main theme from 'The Geese & The Ghost' was briefly considered for use as a theme for a children's TV programme – thus, this mix was done with this purpose in mind. It never came to pass, but the so-called 'kiddies mix' from 1975 is presented here. The woodwind section is to the fore and this brings out the rich melodicism of Ant's writing. I particularly like the delicious reverb treatment on the flute – utterly gorgeous! It ends after two minutes with some guitar chording and a timpani roll.

'Which Way The Wind Blows' (Phillips)
This alternate version of the song finds Ant's original vocals instead of the later overdubs by Phil Collins. It follows the arrangement found on the album, but instrumentally, has just Ant on guitar and bass, while Mike Rutherford provides guitar and a touch of glockenspiel.

'Rowey Song' (Phillips)
This 1972 recording features Ant on his John Bailey six-string guitar as his strumming morphs into some arpeggio picking. Recorded at Send Barns in the winter of that year, it was unearthed from Ant's tape archive in 1997 to be presented here. It's very much a rhythm track awaiting overdubs, but the sequence has a nice feel.

'Lucy Will' (demo) (Phillips)
An August 1978 demo, this is another of Ant's love songs, dedicated to his beloved vanished ballerina, Lucy. It's a great song and the tricky time signatures are already in place and ready to be polished up for its standout inclusion on the 1979 album *Sides*.

'God If I Saw Her Now' (demo) (Phillips)
The side one closer of *The Geese & The Ghost*, this is the original demo of the song that later provided a duet between Phil Collins and Viv McAuliffe. Here, Ant provides both vocal parts on this demo recorded at Send Barns on 28 and 29 July 1970, just over a week after he quit Genesis. He plays all the guitar parts, following the same arrangement as the eventual album version.

'In Memoriam Ad' (Phillips)
The earliest available version of what later became the celebrated 12-string workout 'Reaper', this version was recorded at Send Barns in August 1970.

Harry Williamson and Dave Rootes assisted during this session. The recording opens with the familiar rhythmic, harmonic chording with some fine electric guitar lines moving gently over the strummed backing. The structure of the later *Private Parts & Pieces* track is firmly in place at this early stage, and it remains one of Ant's finest 12-string compositions.

'Hunt Song' (Phillips)

Recorded at Send Barns in the summer of 1977, 'Hunt Song' is the original demo of what later became 'Now What (Are They Doing To My Little Friends?)', the closing track of the 1978 album *Wise After The Event*. Ant performs this demo solely on his acoustic guitars, with a touch of Mellotron. Some of the lyrics are slightly different, and his vocals foster a more intimate feel than the album version.

'Rule Britannia Closing Theme' (Phillips)

Sounding suitably grand with its synth fanfares, string synth melodies and equally synthesized bass intrusions, this closing theme to *Rule Britannia*, the 1981 ITV series on upper-crust Britain, was recorded at Logorhythm Studios on 27 November 1980. All the synth parts are performed by Ant (see chapter on *1984* for commentary on further music from this TV soundtrack).

'Exocet' (Phillips, Scott)

This is basically the instrumental backing for the *Invisible Men* song and there are a few additional parts. The bare instrumental underlines the creeping menace evoked by this unusual 1982 recording. The Mellotron string chords stand out more here than on the vocal version, while the throbbing synthesized bass line exacerbates the ghostly feel of the track. It would make ideal soundtrack material for an ocean-going action film.

'Study In G' (Phillips)

This formal guitar study in G major is in 6/8 time and is a busy-sounding composition that was part of Ant's collection of 1978 classical guitar pieces. Recorded at Send Barns in July of that year, the fast arpeggios that open it give way to more reflective picking with some delicate lines. It returns to a faster picking section with an ascending feel to it.

'Holy Deadlock' (vocal mix) (Phillips, Hall)

This is an interesting experiment from the *Sides* sessions. It takes the chorus from 'Holy Deadlock' with a vocal- and percussion-only mix and repeats it throughout the track. Some decent harmony singing and great percussive intrusions by Ray Cooper (Elton John's long-time percussionist) highlight some hollow woodblocks, a cabasa and a prominent tambourine, along with the vocalising. Instead of the fade-out of the album version, it also sticks with the natural studio ending, where the vocals become more humorous with various vocalised 'bom-boms' and general mayhem as the track peters out – good fun!

'Catch You When You Fall' (Phillips)

Another interesting outtake from the *Sides* sessions is this previously unreleased recording, originally intended as a song until Ant decided the lyrics weren't cutting it. They are, therefore, absent on this instrumental mix that demonstrates the obvious potential of this neglected tune. Recorded at Essex and Matrix Studios over the October/November 1978 period, the unbeatable rhythm section of John G. Perry on his Wal custom bass and Mike Giles on drums again demonstrate their telepathic rapport on this pop-oriented arrangement that sports a driving bass line, close to the one later employed by Genesis for the first half of their 1981 song 'Abacab'. It has a looser-sounding second section, with excellent rhythm and lead guitar from Ant. It's a tidy little sequence that would've made a nifty pop song – it's crying out for lyrics and it's a pity Ant didn't come up with a satisfactory set of alternate lyrics to complete this promising track.

'F Sharp' (Phillips, Rutherford)

Possibly the most famous demo featured here, 'F Sharp' is, of course, the 1969 Phillips/Rutherford demo that would provide the foundation for the Genesis classic 'The Musical Box', the opening track of their 1971 album *Nursery Cryme*. Amazingly, almost every idea employed in that final masterpiece of progressive rock is suggested in this humble demo, on which the top three strings of Ant's and Mike's 12-string guitars are tuned to F#. Combined, the twin 12-string guitars create a peculiar allure, captured so perfectly in the later *Nursery Cryme* track. It's the duo's F# tuning that conjures the magic that's clearly detectable in this historic demo and it proves how much of the final composition was already in place at this Send Barns session in 1969. The spellbinding opening sequence is already intact, followed at 0.13 by the passages that would later comprise the first two verses. The choruses, too, are already in place, commencing at 1.03. It's over this section that Steve Hackett would later add his imitative 'musical box' guitar parts on the Nursery Cryme track. Even the section later employed as the first energised middle variation is firmly in place here, running from 1.15 to 2.11. The final sequence on the 'F Sharp' demo that would appear in the completed version of 'The Musical Box' is the nursery rhyme-inspired 'Old King Cole was a merry old soul...' section.

Elements of 'F Sharp' were also included as part of the composition 'Manipulation', from the 9 January 1970 BBC recording for the documentary intended to illustrate painter Mick Jackson's artwork. It's fascinating to ponder whether working with Jackson's erotic artwork fed into any of the later Peter Gabriel lyrics, which display strong sexual undercurrents (for example, 'The Musical Box', 'The Fountain Of Salmacis' and much of The Lamb Lies Down On Broadway). The band's 1970 recording of 'Manipulation' is available on the 2007 *Genesis 1970-1975* box set as part of the sequence 'Genesis Plays Jackson'. For Genesis fans, the 'F Sharp' demo is in 'goose bump' territory and is a real slice of progressive rock history – listen and be awed!

'The Geese & The Ghost' (Phillips, Rutherford)
This was recorded at the same session as 'F Sharp' – a fortnight-long Genesis rehearsal at Send Barns between 22 September and 3 October 1969. This was prior to their first-ever live Genesis performance, which took place at Garth House in Chobham, Surrey, on 26 October. It was set up by a certain Mrs Balme to celebrate her son Anthony's 21st birthday (which was on the following day). During these rehearsals, Ant and Mike took the opportunity to demo some of their latest compositions via friend Nick Lewin's tape recorder (allowing primitive overdubbing) and one of these was a number known as 'D Instrumental'. This is that very recording, which later became the title track of Ant's first album, *The Geese & The Ghost*.

The 1969 demo shows how complete this piece already was, and under different circumstances, it could have become a Genesis classic, perhaps with the addition of some suitably surreal Peter Gabriel lyrics! However, that wasn't to be the case, so this marvellous composition eventually found a happy home to kick off Ant's solo career eight years later. Ant and Mike's twin 12-strings mesh into that distinctive early-Genesis sound as they negotiate the interlocking themes that would later be bolstered by warm woodwind and keyboard arrangements. This demo makes for a fascinating listen, as the structure of the piece is amazingly complete, even at this early stage.

'F Sharp 2' (Phillips, Rutherford)
The third surviving demo from the 1969 Send Barns sessions featured on CD one, this again sees the two guitarists employing the F# tuning, so effectively used on their first demo in this key. With energetic guitar strumming, this rhythmic second F# demo bears no relation to its more famous cousin but is still a sequence that showed good potential for a possible song. It moves into a slower strummed passage before some single note jiggling sets it back up for another more rhythmic bout of guitar.

'Rowey Reprise' (Phillips)
The reprise of a piece heard earlier features some nice meshing guitars, all played by Ant, along with lightly picked electric guitar lines. Recorded at Send Barns in the winter of 1972.

'Slow Dance' (Phillips)
The 1998 release of *Archive Collection Volume I* marked the first appearance of Ant's attempt to distil the essence of *Slow Dance* into a single format, covered earlier in this text (see chapter on *Slow Dance*).

'The Burnt-Out Cattle Truck Hits The Road' (Phillips)

This 18-second sound experiment was recorded at Vic's Place in January 1991 and was created for potential use on an audio-visual project. Sounding very much like a reversed-tape effect, it's an unusual little trinket.

'The Women Were Watching' (Phillips, Scott)

Recorded at Vic's Place and Atmosphere Studios, the final track on CD one of the Esoteric Records box set *Archive Collection Volume I & Volume II* is basically the instrumental backing track to the Phillips/Scott song inspired by the Falklands conflict. It exposes elements of the arrangement and Jonathan Snowdon's nautical piccolo lines stand out, as does Ant's treated guitar picking. It's slightly longer than the album version and allows some of Ant's fuzz bass improvisations to be appreciated, especially towards the end of the track.

'KIP PJ' (Phillips)

CD two kicks off with this 31-second variation on a previously unheard song. Recorded at Send Barns in the summer of 1978, this snippet consists of guitars and vocals by Ant, recorded via tape reversal.

'Queen Bettine' (Phillips, Rutherford)

Another of the songs from the very early period of Genesis, 'Queen Bettine' was composed by the Genesis duo in December 1968 and was included as part of the original Send Barns demo sessions during September 1969. This version, however, was recorded at the same location but in the summer of 1972, with Ant playing a Zemaitis 12-string, on loan from Mike Rutherford, and providing the charming vocals. With its delicate chording and gently undulating melody, the song evinces a folk/medieval feel, enhanced by the mythical vibe of the lyrics. The strummed choruses are strong, as Ant sings passionately, 'Now is the time to be free'. Complete with a short but nifty 12-string instrumental workout, the song displays a nice balance and is another that could easily have ended up in the Genesis canon.

'What Is The Meaning?' (Phillips, Rutherford)

Returning to the September 1969 Send Barns demo sessions, we're treated to another potential Genesis contender with a title that asks the question of all questions – 'What Is The Meaning?'. The presence of these 1969 demos means that, for any serious Genesis collector, *Archive Collection Volume I & Volume II* is an absolute 'must have' box set. Another of the prolific Genesis duo's late 1960s songs, here we encounter churning acoustic guitars with suspended chords a-plenty to open proceedings, moving to gentler picking that distinctly recalls the picked intro to the Genesis *Trespass* track 'Dusk'. There is also an impressively tight, fast triplet-based picking section, with Ant and Mike panned out to either side of the stereo mix. It's another classic example of the duo's twin guitar technique developing during the early Genesis era. Ant also overdubbed some organ chords to support the twin-guitar matrix.

'Farewell' (Phillips, Rutherford)
The previous track runs straight into this next selection from the September 1969 demos. Another recording based on their familiar twin guitar mesh, this just needed a strong top line and some lyrics to flesh out the initial idea. Towards the end, it becomes gentler and slower. There were so many great ideas being bandied around at this juncture in Genesis history – an endlessly fascinating period for Genesis fans to reflect on.

'Cradle Song' (Phillips)
Now, this is a real gem of a track. It's a substantial, beautifully recorded piano piece running for a surprisingly lengthy 9.04. Initially, it's a triple-time piano lullaby that sounds ideal for rocking a baby to sleep. However, the charming opening sequence soon develops into one of Ant's major piano pieces as tempo and time signature changes see it develop in a wholly organic way, with subtle modulations at key points, along with great use of the piano pedal. It's a quality piece and would've sounded quite at home on Ant's 1986 piano-based *Ivory Moon* album. There's impressive movement from both Ant's right and left hands, especially some flowery runs on the lower end of the keyboard. It moves to some bigger concerto-like chording around the five-minute mark, meaning the baby would probably have woken up by now! But the dynamics of this piece are exquisite and supremely well-judged. It was recorded at Send Barns in July 1978, although the piece itself was initially written in 1972. It's a definite highlight on CD two of the *Archive Collection*.

'Master Of Time' (instrumental version) (Phillips)
This session from August 1973 was recorded using two Revox two-track tape recorders with primitive overdubbing. It's an instrumental take of one of Ant's finest early songs. Laid out instrumentally, it does display the inherent beauty of the song's chord sequence, and this recording is a combination of two separate sections. Personally, listening to this, I do miss Ant's excellent lyrics, but as a variation on the vocal version, it's a track that's still well worth having. The second section features some particularly intense rhythmic scrubbing on guitar.

'Lucy: An Illusion' (Phillips)
A song previously released in a 1990 version on the Virgin Records rerelease of *Private Parts & Pieces II*, the recording here is from a March 1978 session at Send Barns. Ant's vocal displays a wonderful clarity to it as he accompanies himself with an acoustic guitar. It remains a touchingly simple but elegant example of his vintage 1969 songwriting style.

'Henry Goes To War' (Phillips, Rutherford)
Presented here is the 1975 'guitars only' mix of this excerpt from *The Geese & The Ghost* track 'Henry: Portraits From Tudor Times'. It brings out the dynamic between the scrubbed rhythm guitar sections – with their energetic portrayal of Henry VIII's troops galloping off to battle with the French contingent – and the quieter picking sections that, in this setting, bring to mind the timbre employed on parts of the improvisatory section of King Crimson's 'Moonchild' from the 1969 album *In The Court Of The Crimson King*.

'Sleepfall Celeste' (Phillips)
This unique mix of shimmering string chords and tinkling celeste brings out the beauty in this mix of the closing part of 'Sleepfall: The Geese Fly West', the final segment on side two of *The Geese & The Ghost*. The gorgeous string sound is a combination of Ant playing both a hired string synthesiser and Genesis' keyboardist Tony Banks' Mellotron, on loan to Ant for this 6 December 1976 session at Olympic Studios, prior to Banks taking it out on the road for Genesis' *Wind & Wuthering* tour. The bell-like celeste was part of the studio equipment at Olympic.

'God If I Saw Her Now' (Phillips)
Yet another alternate variant on the closing track to side one of *The Geese & The Ghost* presents the interesting vocal combination of Viv McAuliffe and a double-tracked Ant. Accompanied solely by Ant's guitar matrix, it's a touching rendition to listen to as Ant harmonises with himself in reply to Viv McAuliffe's vocalising. This vocal mix was completed at Argonaut Galleries in July 1975.

'Make The Best Of A Bad Situation' (Phillips, Battle)
Ant had previously worked with After The Fire bassist Nick Battle on the production of the 1982 Iva Twydell album *Duel*. 'Make The Best Of A Bad Situation' was recorded in May of that year at Englewood Studios and is basically a piano backing track of the song's chord sequence. As such, it doesn't add up to a great deal, but the chord sequence shows potential for a decent pop tune.

'Regrets' (Phillips)
Recorded at CBS Studios on 6 December 1977 is this initial orchestral run-through for Ant's ballad from *Wise After The Event*. It exposes the impressive orchestral arrangement (all of Ant's own work) and brings out the poignancy of the song's chord sequence. It's taken at a slightly slower tempo than the finished track.

'Nightmare Link' (Phillips)
This short link, running for 52 seconds, features Ant on guitar-synth and has been isolated from the finished track. A wall of shimmering sound is backed

by some keening guitar-synth notes on this brief segment of minutiae from the *Sides* album.

'Greenhouse' (instrumental mix) (Phillips, Gilbert)

The crack rhythm section of Vic Stench and Humbert Ruse are exposed in all their glory once more on this instrumental mix of the whimsical *Wise After The Event* track. Also featuring Jeremy Gilbert on keyboards, the trio cook up a tight, disciplined sound and it's fascinating to study the arrangement *sans* the vocals.

'In Absentia' (Phillips)

Recorded in the summer of 1971, this early collaboration with Harry Williamson was recorded in the attic of friend Mike Pallis' house on a Bang & Olufsen Beochord tape recorder, providing a sound-on-sound overdubbing facility. The results echo the duo's 12-string graphic equalizer experimentation heard on 'Tibetan Yak Music' from *Private Parts & Pieces*. It has a wonderful, treated 12-string sound that is vibrant and alive. This 12-string improvisation by Ant later provided the basis for his proposed 12-string concerto that led to the monster 12-string workout 'Flamingo' on *Private Parts & Pieces*. Some of the themes Ant came up with here also ended up on the same album's 'Field Of Eternity'.

'Stranger' (Phillips, Rutherford)

Of great interest to Genesis fans is this demo, recorded at Send Barns in August 1970, of a song that resided in the Genesis live set for a while, back in 1969, where it was affectionately known as 'Strangler'! It proved too introspective a song to continue playing to live audiences and was dropped as the band learnt about set pacing and coping with a live audience. I previously discussed this song in the chapter on *Private Parts & Pieces*, as Ant's 1990 remake was a bonus track on the 2010 Voiceprint Records rerelease of that album.

The version featured here was recorded much closer to the birth of the song, only a month after Ant quit Genesis. It has a more upfront vocal than the later version, backed by lightly played guitar with some clinking piano notes overdubbed towards the end. Dave Rootes provides some subtle recorder playing and an atmospheric organ chord emerges from the mix as the song concludes. Interestingly, on the *Archive Collection Volume I & Volume II* sleeve notes, the composition is credited solely to Ant, but the Voiceprint bonus track version was credited to both Ant and Mike, which seems more likely to be the case, considering the song's genesis! It's another recording done on the B&O Beochord 'sound-on-sound' tape recorder, hence the rather primitive sound quality.

'Master Of Creation' (Phillips)

This recording, from the iconic September 1969 Genesis rehearsal/demo sessions at Send Barns, proves that the music for Ant's later song, 'Master Of

Time', was alive and well in 1969. Playing piano, Ant works through the sequence that later makes up the verses of the much-loved later track. There's also some overdubbed guitar picking and a more strident piano passage that hints at the later intro of 'Bleak House' from *Sides*. This excerpt from the 1969 sessions fades out after 3.35.

'Pennsylvania Flickhouse' (Phillips)

The oldest artefact by far on this collection, 'Pennsylvania Flickhouse' is indeed the legendary summer 1966 demo by The Anon. It's fascinating to finally hear this slice of Ant's recording history. While the England footballers were in the process of winning the World Cup, the five-piece lineup of The Anon were ensconced in Tony Pike Sound Studios doing their best imitation of The Rolling Stones! Despite Ant and Mike's disappointment over engineer Tony Pike's efforts to tame down their sound, 'Pennsylvania Flickhouse' still exudes a satisfying degree of raunch, as the band plough an impressive R&B groove in tribute to Jagger & Co. Richard Macphail lives up to his Jagger-inspired nickname Mick Phail, while a more-than-decent bluesy riff powers the performance along. For a fledgling band, it's not bad at all and there's even a tidy R&B-style guitar solo from Ant, supported by Mike Rutherford's rhythmic guitar chops. The rhythm section, consisting of the impossibly cool Rivers Job on bass and Rob Tyrell on drums, nail down the beat on a song that Mike Rutherford has described as 'a sort of Godalming Route 66'. The Stones influence is undeniable, but you can see why The Anon were rated as one of the best live Charterhouse bands back in the day – a thoroughly enjoyable bash and a slice of rock history to boot! The group name is often referred to as Anon (as it is in the sleeve notes here), but according to Mike Rutherford, the definite article was added at the time because it sounded cool. The Anon was also stencilled on Rob Tyrell's bass drum skin.

Archive Collection Volume II

'Guitar Song' (Phillips)
Another master unearthed from the Send Barns sessions in the summer of 1973, it's another of Ant's sequences that showed potential as a song but remains here as a guitar backing track. Panned towards one side of the stereo picture, it opens with tasty fingerpicking, morphing into more rhythmic strumming until it fades after 1.58.

'The Anthem From Tarka' (Phillips, Heyworth)
Recorded at Vic's Place in February 1988, this is a combo of two different mixes of the demo for the *Tarka* anthem. A collaboration with Simon Heyworth, it features the lovely melody drawn from the 'Corncrake Meadow' section of *Tarka*. Ant plays keyboards over the basic drum box beat.

'Deep In The Night' (Phillips, Rutherford)
This is another Phillips/Rutherford song from 1969, presented here in instrumental form, as recorded by Ant at Send Barns in August 1977. It was on the shortlist for inclusion on *Wise After The Event* but didn't make the final cut. Fading in, Ant's guitar playing displays picking, strumming and occasional harmonics as the piece negotiates another of the sequences the duo were exploring as potential Genesis songs back in 1969. There are some light electric guitar doodles, but the whole thing feels somewhat underdeveloped.

'Bleak House' (instrumental mix) (Phillips)
Basically, this is the bare piano backing track to one of Ant's major ballads from *Sides*. It still makes for an interesting listen and certainly shows off the magnificent structure of the song, with its rhythmic quirks and sweeping grandiosity.

'Our Man In Japan' (Phillips)
This library piece, recorded at Atmosphere Studios in the summer of 1979, consists of lightly flanged 12-string guitar and bears a strong, stylistic relationship to Ant's fabulous 12-string workout in the middle section of the track 'Wise After The Event'. There are occasional hints of the ambience of the land of the rising sun within this performance, as you might surmise from the title. Also, it's a companion piece to 'Tierra Del Fuego' (see chapter on *Missing Links Volume One: Finger Painting*).

'Child Song' (Phillips)
Written in July 1970, the subtitle of this song is 'A Prayer For Us All' and it was recorded with engineering and production assistance from Mike Rutherford at a Send Barns session in summer 1973. Essentially a child's eye view of Christian beliefs, it comes over with a naïve charm, touchingly sung

by Ant to slow piano chords. There are some subtle guitar overdubs and the piano sound on the fade is a definite nod back to the feel of *From Genesis To Revelation*.

'Old Wives Tale' (Phillips)

This is a composition included on Ant's 1982 album collaboration with Enrique Berro Garcia, *Antiques*. The recording here, though, is an earlier solo version performed on guitar by Ant. Recorded at Send Barns in the summer heatwave of 1976, its plaintive sequence still exudes a tenderness that gives this listener a warm, fuzzy feeling in the stomach on every listen. Composed in 1968, it's basically the instrumental version of the Genesis song 'Little Leaf' – it's marvellous!

'Scottish Suite II' (Phillips, Rutherford)

Working as a kind of sequel to 'Scottish Suite' on *Private Parts & Pieces II* comes this eight-part version, including most of the additional music written by Ant for the aborted *Macbeth* project (see chapters on *Private Parts & Pieces I & II*). The opening section is titled 'Leaping Salmon' and was recorded at Send Barns in the summer of 1973; the rest of this suite was recorded in the summer of 1976. It proceeds via a series of piano triplets with slower changing chords backing them up, after which we're into piano arpeggios as on the *Private Parts & Pieces II* version, but minus the rock rhythm section featured on that version. Staying with just piano while the structure builds, there are some very deep, underpinning left-hand notes before the whole thing moves to a higher octave. A degree of deceleration then moves the piece to high, slow arpeggios.

The second section is titled 'The Witching Hour', its title nodding to the *Macbeth* connection. Here, a spreading organ chord fades into some downward guitar strums supported by several tight snare rolls from drummer Andy McCulloch, introducing Ant's fast guitar triplets, along with a slower, strolling bass end and some mysterious whistling synth notes (all very witchy!). The many dynamic dips give this piece a fascinating flow. According to the sleeve notes, Ralph Bernascone makes another of his cameo appearances here, this time on broomstick!

Part three is titled 'Two Truths' – Mike Rutherford's fuzz bass dominates this short 1.19 segment, recorded at Olympic Studios in June 1976. He also co-wrote the next section with Ant, entitled 'The Letter' (no relation to the much-covered Wayne Carson Thompson song of the same name). It's a fine piano melody, played slowly and reflectively, with a pedal effect on the piano.

'Walpurgis Night' marks the creepy-sounding fifth section with its psychedelic synth sounds running from speaker to speaker, along with plentiful reverse-tape effects. As the synths swish and swirl across the sound picture, it makes for a spooky interlude and a galvanising listening experience.

The loveliest section for me is 'Sweet Reaper', another excerpt from Ant's wonderful 12-string classic, 'Reaper' (see chapter on *Private Parts & Pieces*). His guitar here sounds truly gorgeous, and the melodiousness of this section makes it an obvious highlight. It sounds as if the guitar is being shadowed by a piano-like sound, but, knowing Ant's ability on 12-string, this could well be generated on just that one instrument.

The intriguingly titled seventh section of this suite, 'Why Sinks This Cauldron?', is a brief 44-second guitar link of slow, rhythmic chording, leading to the finale, 'Her Last Sleepwalk', where a shimmering sound fades to a reverb-rich piano arpeggio to close 'Scottish Suite II' after a further 46 seconds.

'Sally' (instrumental mix) (Phillips)

An instrumental version of the backing track for one of the highlights of *Invisible Men*, this mix shows off the big synth intro chords, leading into a drum box rhythm. It's a fabulous sequence that, once furnished with Ant's lyrics, provided an absolute highlight to this pop-oriented 1983 album. This is the eight-track version recorded at Englewood Studios prior to overdubs being added at Atmosphere Studios.

'Windmill' (Phillips)

Recorded at Send Barns in the autumn of 1971, this free and easy-sounding pin piano piece received a thumbs-up from Send Barns visitor Peter Gabriel, who admired its free movement. Ant placed drawing pins under the hammers to achieve the distinctive sound heard here. It's a free improvisation, edited from a longer recording.

'Tregenna Afternoons' (demo) (Phillips)

This early demo of Ant's Cornish soundscape heard on *Private Parts & Pieces* moves in gentle waves of picking, moving to a faster tempo three minutes in. Of note on this version is his use of the Fender Stratocaster electric guitar to conjure some tasteful wah-wah effects beneath the acoustic guitar matrix. Recorded at Send Barns in the summer of 1973, this version features an end section that's missing on the later recording. Still redolent of pasties, piskies, tin mines and North Cornwall ruggedness, this pastoral tribute to Kernow closes at 7.41.

'Lofty Vaults' (Phillips)

Perhaps inspired by gazing towards the ceiling of a particularly ornate cathedral, 'Lofty Vaults' is propped up by some big, churchy organ chords underpinned by grand bass pedal notes. The cathedral-like vibe is strong on this 1.21 library piece from a summer 1979 session at Atmosphere Studios.

'Variation On A Theme Of Fantomas' (Phillips)

In the autumn of 1973, Ant's friend Philip Black requested a soundtrack for a student film he was producing, based on a character created by two French

126

writers, Marcel Allain and Pierre Souvestre, back in 1911: Fantomas. This character, inspired by the work of Belgian Surrealist Rene Magritte, was an evil criminal mastermind. Another Send Barns 1973 recording, there is indeed a dastardly feel to some of the piano chording, in some downbeat harmonic choices, although the piece moves upwards to a more hopeful feel in places. Some high tinkling piano runs trip lightly from Ant's fingers at one point, only to descend to gloomier harmonies again in this 5.04 study. Although never used for the film in the end, it's a piece that finds a welcome home here for Ant's many fans to savour.

'Picardy Pictures' (Phillips)
Another of Ant's impressionistic guitar pieces, 'Picardy Pictures' was recorded at Send Barns in the autumn of 1972. It fades in on a stream of guitar arpeggios and seems to fade and return as it wends its way along. It has a lightly dancing feel in places.

'Polar Lights' (Phillips)
Another library piece from the Atmosphere Studios sessions in the summer of 1979, engineer John Reiner does a great job in treating Ant's keyboard sound through the mixing desk, as the swirling keys, overlaying a synth-generated tone, conjure the visual delights of the aurora borealis, also known as the northern lights. This phenomenon is created by the solar wind interacting with Earth's magnetosphere as it ionises particles of different elements, each one giving rise to a contrasting colour.

'The Ridolfi Plot' (Phillips)
A potential song for the *Sides* album, this Send Barns recording from September 1978 never made it onto that album in the end. Running for 6.15, Ant plays his Rudloff eight-string guitar, as the contemplative picking makes use of a return to a prominent bass string, almost giving some passages a pedal feel. There's some nice movement, and the tempo takes off to a degree halfway through. There are some nice changes to enjoy and a high, chorded ending. The title reflects the 1571 Roman Catholic plot to assassinate Queen Elizabeth I and replace her with Mary, Queen of Scots. It was named after international banker Robert Ridolfi, who hatched the diabolical plot.

'Falling For Love' (instrumental mix) (Phillips, Scott)
CD one of *Archive Collection Volume II* closes with another backing track from the 1982 *Invisible Men* sessions in the shape of this instrumental mix of the gorgeous ballad 'Falling For Love', another highlight of that album. It's still a pleasing sequence to listen to, even without the lyrics. It's slow, funky and highly melodic. Driven by electric piano, the highlight here is undoubtedly Ant's electric guitar flourishes, his understated solo and some two-note hammering to close.

'Highland Fling' (Phillips)
The second CD opens with another library piece recorded in the summer of 1979 at Logorhythm Studios. Tight downward guitar strums plot the course of this Scottish-tinged composition, evoking the highland dance variation popularised in the 19th century. With a hand on one hip, the other pointing skywards, and one leg half-cocked up the other leg, we're ready for a quick fling around the living room! A second section of guitar arpeggios accompanied by a high pipe-like synth line adds interest to this pleasant tune.

'Prelude #1' (Phillips)
Decorum returns with this studied classical guitar composition, opening with two-to-the-bar strummed chords and some delicate picking. Laid down at a Send Barns session in the summer of 1981, 'Prelude #1' is a reflective rumination, moving to a higher octave as it progresses.

'Siesta' (Phillips)
From the same session as the previous track, 'Siesta' proves to be a lazily drifting guitar composition with a nice sense of space and a relaxing, reflective vibe, ideal to accompany an afternoon catnap in a hammock. Flickers of guitar harmonics dance like leaves in a gentle breeze and all is sleepily peaceful.

'Bubble & Squeak' (Phillips)
A piece also featured on *Slow Waves, Soft Stars,* this is an earlier recording of Ant's paean to a dish that American food writer Howard Hillman once rather condescendingly referred to as 'one of the great peasant dishes of the world'. Ant's rhythmic guitar chording certainly bubbles along nicely in this recording from the August 1981 Send Barns sessions. Best of all, it closes with a nifty, lightly played, upward-spreading arpeggio, topped by a staccato strike of the final chord that leaves a pleasing reverb afterglow in its wake – superb!

'Guru' (instrumental mix) (Phillips)
Basically, this is the bare backing track for the fine *Invisible Men* song 'Guru' as it was in its eight-track stage at Englewood Studios in the spring of 1982. It shows off the structure of the song to good effect.

'Shady Arbours' (Phillips, Rutherford)
Here we have a touch of spontaneity, captured at Send Barns in October 1974, in the shape of an improvisation by the long-time Phillips/Rutherford team on their 12-string guitars. As one guitar picks over one constant chord, the other guitar features more animated picking. It's always great to hear these two musicians working together in this way. It's a track that fades in at the beginning and fades out at the end after a short duration of 1.46.

'West Side Alice' (Phillips)
This is a piano piece intended for inclusion in the musical *Alice*, although it never did make the final selection for the show. It carries a show-tune vibe, as it starts in a lower octave and moves up a notch as it progresses. Recorded at Vic's Place in November 1983, it slows slightly towards the end and fades after 2.59.

'Vic's Tango' (Phillips)
Who can resist a tango? Not Vic, by the sound of it. Backed with a drum box, Ant's acoustic guitar picks an Argentinian-tinged melody over the dance's distinctive rhythm. Emerging in the 1880s along the Argentine/Uruguayan border, it's a fascinating dance to watch, with its abrupt moves and showy poses. Ant captures its flavour in this short composition that sounds as if it could provide an effective theme tune for a TV show. There are a couple of purposeful nods to the 1954 tango show-tune 'Hernando's Hideaway' (from *The Pajama Game*) – but minus the 'Ole'! Recorded at Vic's Place in April 1983, it's a piece that was composed on piano and pitched for an intended film project. This guitar-based version was demoed for a later audio-visual project. Vic does himself proud here. Good fun all round.

'Seven Long Years' (instrumental mix) (Phillips)
One of Ant's most moving short songs, here we encounter the 1976 instrumental mix of a tune that featured twice on *Private Parts & Pieces*, once as a guitar instrumental ('Lullabye – Old Father Time') and once in its vocal version. This is basically the instrumental backing of the song version. It's a wonderful and moving melody.

'Romeo & Juliet' (Phillips)
Ant's debut library sessions occurred in 1976, and this short piece is from those Send Barns sessions. Two guitars, one strumming and one picking, back some high synth notes on this 34-second snippet.

'I Saw You Today' (Phillips)
This is a 1978 Send Barns remake of a song that was first released in its 1977 version on *Private Parts & Pieces II* in 1980. The version here follows the same arrangement as the earlier reading, as Ant plays his 12-string guitar and sings his song of longing in that uniquely emotional voice of his. The 12-string shimmers in the final verse prior to Ant's exhortations of love that form the coda of this fine song.

'The Anthem From Tarka' (alternate demo mix) (Phillips, Heyworth)
We lose the drum box on this floating keyboard-based version of the first part of 'The Anthem'. The melody's sublime beauty comes through loud and clear in this 1.01 edit.

'Quadrille' (from *Alice*) (Phillips, Scott)

Next up is Ant's demo for an instrumental, written as musical accompaniment for a choreographed number, featured in the Phillips/Scott musical *Alice* during its run at Leeds Playhouse in the spring of 1984. Recorded at Vic's Place in November 1983, this instrumental demo, performed mainly on piano, is based on the dance rhythms of the quadrille, a folk dance popular in Europe from the 18th century onwards. With many abrupt tempo changes and lots of staccato accents, the piano chording is shadowed by some arpeggio synth motifs. It certainly represented a different direction for Ant at the time and worked well within the format of the *Alice* musical. This was the first official release of any of the music from this musical.

'Desert Suite' (Phillips)

Intended for an Atmosphere Music Library audio-visual project about the Middle East, this suite was recorded at Send Barns in June 1980. It's divided into three subtitled sections, the first being 'Sand Dance'. With drum box backing, Ant employs his guitars and keyboards to cook up a sweaty Eastern vibe. There are Arabic scales a-plenty, with fast 12-string riffs and lots of speedy, jiggling guitar notes. It moves into a descending sequence as it progresses. The second part, 'Pipelines', is a nod to the oil industry of the region and the synths here bubble along like the liquid oil in the pipelines – very descriptive. 'End Theme' completes this short suite, as scintillating synth sounds collide with very Arabic-sounding synthesized doodles over organ chords as the suite concludes at 4.33.

'Fantomas (Opening Theme)' (Phillips)

The opening theme for Philip Black's 1973 film project *Fantomas* was recorded at Send Barns in the autumn of that year. For this session, Ant was reunited with his former Genesis bandmate, drummer John Silver. It's built on a foundation of fast piano riffs at the lower end of the keyboard, over which chording at the treble end builds. Pretty much unique in Ant's output, this track exudes a strong jazz swing, mainly due to the jazzy drum style of John Silver. It's a track that's high on atmosphere and really hooks into that early 20th-century silent movie feel. This was the first time Silver had recorded with Ant since the sessions for *From Genesis To Revelation* in the summer of 1968. From this evidence, it's a pity Ant didn't employ the drummer for a complete project going forward – it would have been interesting.

'Sistine' (instrumental mix) (Phillips)

This is an early June 1982 mix from Englewood Studios of the backing track for Ant's wonderful song, which is to be heard in its full glory on *A Catch At The Tables*. You can already hear the potential, even in this early form, but once completed with its later overdubs, it would be something of a masterpiece of songwriting (see chapter on *Private Parts & Pieces IV*).

'Sisters Of Remindum' (basic mix) (Phillips)

The main points of interest in this composite mix of the *Sides* track that graced the opening of side two of the album are Ant's initial piano track – laid down in October 1977 at Mike Giles' studio in Dorset – and the separate second section, which displays the unadorned wonder of the John Perry/Mike Giles rhythm section. The way this duo effortlessly pick their way through the tricky, super-fast 9/8 section of this piece is laid bare in all its magnificence – enjoy the moment!

'Will The Last Man Off The Ice Rink (Please Turn Out The Lights)' (Phillips)

I love the short experimental recording ideas that Ant spontaneously slides in here and there, and this is another of them. With its title reflecting his long-standing energy-saving obsession (check out the final line of the 1979 *Sides* extra, 'Souvenir'), here we have an experiment from a summer 1973 Send Barns session, as he applies heavy tape delay to a piano doodle. There are also a few disembodied 'ahs' in the background, adding to the track's atmosphere – great stuff!

'Finale' (instrumental mix) (Phillips)

Also included on the 2017 *Invisible Men* rerelease on Esoteric Records, I essentially covered this instrumental mix in that chapter. Its first appearance was on the 2004 rerelease of *Archive Collection Volume II*.

The Masquerade Tapes

As previously mentioned, *Masquerade* was a planned musical based on the 1979 Kit Williams book of the same name. It was a book that sparked off a countrywide treasure hunt, as the puzzles and riddles in the book illustrations provided clues to the whereabouts of an 18-carat jewelled pendant of a hare that had been carefully secreted away in a mystery location. The hare represents a central character of the book, Jack Hare, who is tasked with transporting a treasure from the Moon to the Sun, but this trinket goes missing on the journey. Kit Williams' story seemed ripe for a musical adaption, and this set off a long, convoluted train of events that variously involved Ant's manager, Tony Smith, who set about acquiring the theatrical rights to stage the show; producer Rupert Hine, along with his girlfriend, Jeannette Obstoj; keyboardist Rod Argent and, of course, Ant himself. After several years of toing-and-froing, Ant, together with Richard Scott, planned their own musical version of the *Masquerade* concept, collating previous demos recorded by Ant in 1980. Then, in April 1981, the duo headed to Send Barns to start recording additional music composed by Ant around the *Masquerade* idea. Scott's friend, Lindsey Moore, also became involved in the recordings and added vocals to 'Moon's Lament For The Sun'. In one of those weird quirks of Genesis history, vocalist Moore had made her debut as a teenager by providing the title song for the 1969 film *I Start Counting*, which also featured an uncredited appearance of a young Phil Collins! Some of the music on the *Masquerade* tapes was also released in different versions on Ant's 1986 piano album *Private Parts & Pieces VI: Ivory Moon* in the shape of 'Tara's Theme' and 'Moonfall'.

'Overture' (Phillips, Scott)
Providing a suitably dramatic start to proceedings, 'Overture' is just that – a grand thematic statement, opening with some high synth arpeggios, along with a slower, bass-toned melody. Dramatic chord strikes on synthesiser are pinned by an effective bass movement beneath, leading to a series of big, churchy chords. There's some judicious panning going on, keeping the sound picture sharp and clean. Ant's usual synth choices are in evidence, relying on his trusty ARP 2600 and Polymoog keyboards. A guitar picks up the melodic line in a piece that's full of light and shade. 'Overture' is one of the tracks from the April to June 1981 Send Barns sessions.

'Moon' (Phillips, Scott)
The start of Jack Hare's journey, 'Moon' is where he obtains the treasure prior to its transportation to the Sun. The on-beat synth rhythm sets up a pattern as keyboard riffs rise ever higher, starting the long journey to the Sun. It's a piece that shifts time signatures as it proceeds; Ant sprinkles some guitar figures among the synth-based melodies. Towards the end, the synth lines take on a whimsical bent, and prior to arriving at our next track, an uphill melodic sequence leads us straight into 'Sun' after 3.31.

'Sun' (Phillips, Scott)

The Sun is represented by spreading, shimmering synthesiser and some deeper synth notes. The synth sounds are mixed with Ant's guitar sounds here, with a treated 12-string contrasting downward strums with arpeggios to good effect. It's all rather cinematic and widescreen, with piano also joining the mix. At one point, a synth produces an almost bouncy sound, as major/minor variations abound and some widely spread triplets add rhythmic interest. It's at this point in the story that Jack Hare realises the treasure has been lost – its eventual location, once the gold hare pendant was found, was Ampthill Park in Bedfordshire.

'Tara's Theme' (Phillips)

Representing another character from Kit Williams' *Masquerade* book, Tara Treetops, this is a lovely piano melody. Here, it is bolstered by Ant's Roland CR78 drum box, along with some glistening synth chords panned to one side of the stereo picture during the contrasting middle section. It's a romantic and very filmic piece of music. The unadorned piano version is covered in the chapter on *Private Parts & Pieces VI: Ivory Moon*. The version here, though, was recorded five years earlier, in the spring of 1981.

'Craw' (Phillips, Scott)

Missing from the original demos for *Masquerade*, 'Craw' was rerecorded at Vic's Place in November 1983. It's an unusual, music hall-influenced piano piece with a walking bass line on the lower reaches of the keyboard. A contrasting section uses dissonance to good effect and is almost comical, conjuring the image of a cartoon-like character picking their way through a hazardous environment of some kind! Sounding akin to a silent movie-style soundtrack, it's great fun to listen to, and there are some disorienting six-beat phrases that make it sound even more off-kilter. After 2.05, it's edited straight into the next track.

'All Horrors Of The Night' (Phillips)

Carrying forward the strangeness of the piano sounds heard in 'Craw' comes this earlier recording, taped at Send Barns in January 1980. Again, it is very theatrical; the piano playing here is performed at high velocity and is extremely rhythmic in style. After 4.26, the pace starts to falter, only to arrive at a big staccato chord to finish.

'Penny Pockets' (Phillips)

Based on Ant's 12-string guitar, alternately employing slow downward strums and faster arpeggio picking, this is a piece with a very song-like structure. A more speedily picked spread of chords contrasts with the initial sequence, and the piece concludes with a passage that evokes a sinking feeling. This is another of the January 1980 recordings from Send Barns.

'Hare B Minor' (Phillips)

Recorded at the January 1980 Send Barns sessions, the opening passage to this piano-based composition sports some convoluting riffs twisting rapidly beneath the piano chording in the key of B minor (as you might guess from its title). It's a dandy little sequence that modulates to a distinctly classical, cyclic feel with a Bach-like bass end, lending the piece a rather elegant bearing.

'Destiny' (Phillips, Scott)

With piano chords on a crotchet beat and a descending feel to the bass end, this song-like creation bears a strong similarity to the composing style of The Beach Boys' resident musical genius Brian Wilson. It's decorated with some higher synth lines as it progresses. With a wave-like sequence and a classic pop structure, 'Destiny' is crying out for a suitable lyric, which presumably would've been provided by Richard Scott had this music been staged. With its hugely appealing chord structure and solidly logical progression, it's a fabulous piece, even in this incarnation, recorded at the spring/summer 1981 Send Barns sessions.

'Fire' (Phillips)

Another piano piece, the chord spread underlying it brings to my mind some of the music composed by John Barry for the 1960s James Bond films. It contrasts urgent staccato piano chording with a six-beat passage, which recurs several times as the piece builds up. It was recorded at Send Barns in January 1980.

'Yellow Carpet' (Phillips, Scott)

The on-beat crotchet rhythm of 'Yellow Carpet' returns us to a 1960s vibe on this piano-based selection with a whimsical melody that weaves above a guitar/synth section. Again, it's very song-oriented in structure and is probably another one that could've been more complete with some lyrics. Nevertheless, it's still fun to listen to as Ant adds some surprisingly wailing electric guitar lines.

Towards the end, this jaunty confection is driven forward by some bolero-style bass parts, and you can clearly hear both Ant's rhythm and lead guitar parts spread across the sound picture. The recording is from the April to June 1981 Send Barns sessions.

'Masque Moon' (Phillips)

More reflective and calming is 'Masque Moon', a piano contemplation with a slow, gentle movement. Around 2.10, there is a change to a gradual, on-beat piano rhythm before resuming the calm reflection of the opening passage once more.

It was recorded at Send Barns in January 1980.

'Moon's Lament For The Sun' (Phillips, Hine, Scott)
The one track of this collection that is a complete song, here, we are introduced to the vocals of Lindsey Moore, who sings beautifully over a lovely sequence as her vocal slowly tumbles in downward spirals above a gorgeous spread of chords. A repeated contrasting section has a slightly darker feel and a fair degree of poignancy as, over a piano backing, with harpsichord-like arpeggios supporting, Moore beseeches her loved one: 'Hold me, I'm falling'. This affecting love song reflects a resigned sadness, especially her closing line of 'I've lost your love'. It's a truly gorgeous song, recorded at the April to June 1981 Send Barns sessions.

'Last Of The Heavy Hares' (Phillips, Scott)
Some brief introductory vocoder doodles soon move to the fast, synth-driven beat that quickly doubles time. The whole track has the same vibe as much of Ant's *1984* album, mainly due to the ARP 2600 and Polymoog synthesisers, I would guess. It was recorded at Send Barns a few months after Ant had completed that album in the first half of 1981. It sports bubbling synth breaks and an effervescent demeanour, including some synth triplets, harmony line sections and scuttering synth overlay, with a busy feel.

'Only A Dream' (Phillips, Scott)
The finale of *Masquerade*, 'Only A Dream' sits upon a drum box rhythm and is propelled by some galloping acoustic guitar chords and chordal picking. It's a lively piece that contrasts the two guitar styles to good effect. There are some electric guitar lines low in the mix and the arpeggio-picking section recurring towards the end is decorated by a synth line with a strong familiarity with the *Invisible Men* album. It's the melody that forms the 'traces of you' part, employed as a chant of those words at the end of the chorus on the song 'Traces', from the aforementioned album, which was recorded the year after 'Only A Dream' was committed to tape at Send Barns in April/June 1981.

Additional Material
'Sir Isaac' (Phillips)
This piano piece intended for the *Masquerade* project was recorded at Send Barns in the January 1980 sessions and remained unreleased until Esoteric Records' 2016 rerelease of *Private Parts & Pieces V-VIII*. It turned up on the extra CD with this set, *Private Parts & Extra Pieces II*. It's a contemplative piece with some nice movement and modulations. It bears the hallmarks of Ant's favoured logical style of composition in the classical mould. I'm not quite sure where it fitted into the *Masquerade* musical that wasn't to be. From the title, astronomer and mathematician (and inventor of the reflecting telescope) Sir Isaac Newton is instantly evoked. 'Sir Isaac's ineffable logic certainly reflects Newton's personality. The piece moves to some higher chording, then slows to a degree towards its close.

Anthony Phillips 1977-1990 ... *On Track*

'The Princess Waltz' (Phillips)

This little gem didn't turn up until the CD *Private Parts & Extra Pieces* was made available by Esoteric Records, along with the 2015 box set *Private Parts & Pieces I-IV*. I've placed it here as it's another planned composition for the *Masquerade* project that was recorded at the Send Barns January 1980 sessions. As the title suggests, it's a charming waltz with a stately bearing. The piano carries the main thrust of the triple-time rhythm, but the smooth bass lines give the piece a terpsichorean glide, backed up with supporting guitar and delicious employment of tinkling glockenspiel, conjuring the sparkling dress of a waltzing Princess. It's a track that's atmospherically redolent of pumpkin coaches and glass slippers: 'You *will* go to the ball, Cinderella!'

Afterword

Following the artistic triumph of *Slow Dance* in 1990, Ant went on to have a fruitful and productive career through the 1990s and into the 21st century, but sadly, dear reader, there we must leave it. Ant's later career will need to be another tale for another volume. Happily, both the *Private Parts & Pieces* and *Missing Links* series continued going forward. At the time of writing, the former series now has 12 volumes, and the latter has four volumes. There have also been various album releases of Ant's compositions for library, TV and film work, along with some excellent main sequence albums. The ex-Genesis guitarist remains a uniquely creative and imaginative musician whose continuing output will always be worthy of a close listen. For details on later Anthony Phillips releases, I refer you to his informative website – *anthonyphillips.co.uk* – which is well worth checking out for lovers of Ant's music and Genesis fans in general.

Also available from Sonicbond

On Track series
AC/DC – Chris Sutton 978-1-78952-307-2
Allman Brothers Band – Andrew Wild 978-1-78952-252-5
Tori Amos – Lisa Torem 978-1-78952-142-9
Aphex Twin – Beau Waddell 978-1-78952-267-9
Asia – Peter Braidis 978-1-78952-099-6
Badfinger – Robert Day-Webb 978-1-878952-176-4
Barclay James Harvest – Keith and Monica Domone 978-1-78952-067-5
Beck – Arthur Lizie 978-1-78952-258-7
The Beat, General Public, Fine Young Cannibals – Steve Parry 978-1-78952-274-7
The Beatles 1962-1996 – Alberto Bravin and Andrew Wild 978-1-78952-355-3
The Beatles Solo 1969-1980 – Andrew Wild 978-1-78952-030-9
Blue Oyster Cult – Jacob Holm-Lupo 978-1-78952-007-1
Blur – Matt Bishop 978-178952-164-1
Marc Bolan and T.Rex – Peter Gallagher 978-1-78952-124-5
David Bowie 1964 to 1982 – Carl Ewens 978-1-78952-324-9
David Bowie 1963 to 2016 – Don Klees 978-1-78952-351-5
Kate Bush – Bill Thomas 978-1-78952-097-2
The Byrds – Andy McArthur 978-1-78952-280-8
Camel – Hamish Kuzminski 978-1-78952-040-8
Captain Beefheart – Opher Goodwin 978-1-78952-235-8
Caravan – Andy Boot 978-1-78952-127-6
Cardiacs – Eric Benac 978-1-78952-131-3
Wendy Carlos – Mark Marrington 978-1-78952-331-7
The Carpenters – Paul Tornbohm 978-1-78952-301-0
Nick Cave and The Bad Seeds – Dominic Sanderson 978-1-78952-240-2
Eric Clapton Solo – Andrew Wild 978-1-78952-141-2
The Clash (revised edition) – Nick Assirati 978-1-78952-325-6
Elvis Costello and The Attractions – Georg Purvis 978-1-78952-129-0
Crosby, Stills and Nash – Andrew Wild 978-1-78952-039-2
Creedence Clearwater Revival – Tony Thompson 978-1-78952-237-2
Crowded House – Jon Magidsohn 978-1-78952-292-1
The Damned – Morgan Brown 978-1-78952-136-8
David Bowie 1964 to 1982 – Carl Ewens 978-1-78952-324-9
David Bowie 1964 to 1982 – Carl Ewens 978-1-78952-324-9
Deep Purple and Rainbow 1968-79 – Steve Pilkington 978-1-78952-002-6
Deep Purple from 1984 – Phil Kafcaloudes 978-1-78952-354-6
Depeche Mode – Brian J. Robb 978-1-78952-277-8
Dire Straits – Andrew Wild 978-1-78952-044-6
The Divine Comedy – Alan Draper 978-1-78952-308-9
The Doors – Tony Thompson 978-1-78952-137-5
Dream Theater – Jordan Blum 978-1-78952-050-7
Bob Dylan 1962-1970 – Opher Goodwin 978-1-78952-275-2
Eagles – John Van der Kiste 978-1-78952-260-0
Earth, Wind and Fire – Bud Wilkins 978-1-78952-272-3
Electric Light Orchestra – Barry Delve 978-1-78952-152-8
Emerson Lake and Palmer – Mike Goode 978-1-78952-000-2
Fairport Convention – Kevan Furbank 978-1-78952-051-4

Also available from Sonicbond

Peter Gabriel – Graeme Scarfe 978-1-78952-138-2
Genesis – Stuart MacFarlane 978-1-78952-005-7
Gentle Giant – Gary Steel 978-1-78952-058-3
Gong – Kevan Furbank 978-1-78952-082-8
Green Day – William E. Spevack 978-1-78952-261-7
Steve Hackett – Geoffrey Feakes 978-1-78952-098-9
Hall and Oates – Ian Abrahams 978-1-78952-167-2
Peter Hammill – Richard Rees Jones 978-1-78952-163-4
Roy Harper – Opher Goodwin 978-1-78952-130-6
Hawkwind (new edition) – Duncan Harris 978-1-78952-290-7
Jimi Hendrix – Emma Stott 978-1-78952-175-7
The Hollies – Andrew Darlington 978-1-78952-159-7
Horslips – Richard James 978-1-78952-263-1
The Human League and The Sheffield Scene – Andrew Darlington 978-1-78952-186-3
Humble Pie –Robert Day-Webb 978-1-78952-2761
Ian Hunter – G. Mick Smith 978-1-78952-304-1
The Incredible String Band – Tim Moon 978-1-78952-107-8
INXS – Manny Grillo 978-1-78952-302-7
Iron Maiden – Steve Pilkington 978-1-78952-061-3
Joe Jackson – Richard James 978-1-78952-189-4
The Jam – Stan Jeffries 978-1-78952-299-0
Jefferson Airplane – Richard Butterworth 978-1-78952-143-6
Jethro Tull – Jordan Blum 978-1-78952-016-3
J. Geils Band – James Romag 978-1-78952-332-4
Elton John in the 1970s – Peter Kearns 978-1-78952-034-7
Billy Joel – Lisa Torem 978-1-78952-183-2
Journey – Doug Thornton 978-1-78952-337-9
Judas Priest – John Tucker 978-1-78952-018-7
Kansas – Kevin Cummings 978-1-78952-057-6
Killing Joke – Nic Ransome 978-1-78952-273-0
The Kinks – Martin Hutchinson 978-1-78952-172-6
Korn – Matt Karpe 978-1-78952-153-5
Led Zeppelin – Steve Pilkington 978-1-78952-151-1
Level 42 – Matt Philips 978-1-78952-102-3
Little Feat – Georg Purvis – 978-1-78952-168-9
Magnum – Matthew Taylor – 978-1-78952-286-0
Aimee Mann – Jez Rowden 978-1-78952-036-1
Ralph McTell – Paul O. Jenkins 978-1-78952-294-5
Metallica – Barry Wood 978-1-78952-269-3
Joni Mitchell – Peter Kearns 978-1-78952-081-1
The Moody Blues – Geoffrey Feakes 978-1-78952-042-2
Motorhead – Duncan Harris 978-1-78952-173-3
Nektar – Scott Meze – 978-1-78952-257-0
New Order – Dennis Remmer – 978-1-78952-249-5
Nightwish – Simon McMurdo – 978-1-78952-270-9
Nirvana – William E. Spevack 978-1-78952-318-8
Laura Nyro – Philip Ward 978-1-78952-182-5
Oasis – Andrew Rooney 978-1-78952-300-3

Also available from Sonicbond

Phil Ochs – Opher Goodwin 978-1-78952-326-3
Mike Oldfield – Ryan Yard 978-1-78952-060-6
Opeth – Jordan Blum 978-1-78-952-166-5
Pearl Jam – Ben L. Connor 978-1-78952-188-7
Tom Petty – Richard James 978-1-78952-128-3
Pink Floyd – Richard Butterworth 978-1-78952-242-6
The Police – Pete Braidis 978-1-78952-158-0
Porcupine Tree (Revised Edition) – Nick Holmes 978-1-78952-346-1
Procol Harum – Scott Meze 978-1-78952-315-7
Queen – Andrew Wild 978-1-78952-003-3
Radiohead – William Allen 978-1-78952-149-8
Gerry Rafferty – John Van der Kiste 978-1-78952-349-2
Rancid – Paul Matts 978-1-78952-187-0
Lou Reed 1972-1986 – Ethan Roy 978-1-78952-283-9
Renaissance – David Detmer 978-1-78952-062-0
REO Speedwagon – Jim Romag 978-1-78952-262-4
The Rolling Stones 1963-80 – Steve Pilkington 978-1-78952-017-0
Linda Ronstadt 1969-1989 – Daryl O. Lawrence 987-1-78952-293-8
Roxy Music – Michael Kulikowski 978-1-78952-335-5
Rush 1973 to 1982 – Richard James 978-1-78952-338-6
Sensational Alex Harvey Band – Peter Gallagher 978-1-7952-289-1
The Small Faces and The Faces – Andrew Darlington 978-1-78952-316-4
The Smashing Pumpkins – Matt Karpe 978-1-7952-291-4
The Smiths and Morrissey – Tommy Gunnarsson 978-1-78952-140-5
Soft Machine – Scott Meze 978-1078952-271-6
Sparks 1969-1979 – Chris Sutton 978-1-78952-279-2
Spirit – Rev. Keith A. Gordon – 978-1-78952- 248-8
Stackridge – Alan Draper 978-1-78952-232-7
Status Quo the Frantic Four Years – Richard James 978-1-78952-160-3
Steely Dan – Jez Rowden 978-1-78952-043-9
The Stranglers – Martin Hutchinson 978-1-78952-323-2
Talk Talk – Gary Steel 978-1-78952-284-6
Talking Heads – David Starkey 978-178952-353-9
Tears For Fears – Paul Clark – 978-178952-238-9
Thin Lizzy – Graeme Stroud 978-1-78952-064-4
Tool – Matt Karpe 978-1-78952-234-1
Toto – Jacob Holm-Lupo 978-1-78952-019-4
U2 – Eoghan Lyng 978-1-78952-078-1
UFO – Richard James 978-1-78952-073-6
Ultravox – Brian J. Robb 978-1-78952-330-0
Van Der Graaf Generator – Dan Coffey 978-1-78952-031-6
Van Halen – Morgan Brown – 9781-78952-256-3
Suzanne Vega – Lisa Torem 978-1-78952-281-5
Jack White And The White Stripes – Ben L. Connor 978-1-78952-303-4
The Who – Geoffrey Feakes 978-1-78952-076-7
Roy Wood and the Move – James R Turner 978-1-78952-008-8
Yes (new edition) – Stephen Lambe 978-1-78952-282-2
Neil Young 1963 to 1970 – Oper Goodwin 978-1-78952-298-3

Frank Zappa 1966 to 1979 – Eric Benac 978-1-78952-033-0
Warren Zevon – Peter Gallagher 978-1-78952-170-2
The Zombies – Emma Stott 978-1-78952-297-6
10CC – Peter Kearns 978-1-78952-054-5

Decades Series
The Bee Gees in the 1960s – Andrew Mon Hughes et al 978-1-78952-148-1
The Bee Gees in the 1970s – Andrew Mon Hughes et al 978-1-78952-179-5
Black Sabbath in the 1970s – Chris Sutton 978-1-78952-171-9
Britpop – Peter Richard Adams and Matt Pooler 978-1-78952-169-6
Phil Collins in the 1980s – Andrew Wild 978-1-78952-185-6
Alice Cooper in the 1970s – Chris Sutton 978-1-78952-104-7
Alice Cooper in the 1980s – Chris Sutton 978-1-78952-259-4
Curved Air in the 1970s – Laura Shenton 978-1-78952-069-9
Donovan in the 1960s – Jeff Fitzgerald 978-1-78952-233-4
Bob Dylan in the 1980s – Don Klees 978-1-78952-157-3
Brian Eno in the 1970s – Gary Parsons 978-1-78952-239-6
Faith No More in the 1990s – Matt Karpe 978-1-78952-250-1
Fleetwood Mac in the 1970s – Andrew Wild 978-1-78952-105-4
Fleetwood Mac in the 1980s – Don Klees 978-178952-254-9
Focus in the 1970s – Stephen Lambe 978-1-78952-079-8
Free and Bad Company in the 1970s – John Van der Kiste 978-1-78952-178-8
Genesis in the 1970s – Bill Thomas 978178952-146-7
George Harrison in the 1970s – Eoghan Lyng 978-1-78952-174-0
Kiss in the 1970s – Peter Gallagher 978-1-78952-246-4
Manfred Mann's Earth Band in the 1970s – John Van der Kiste 978178952-243-3
Marillion in the 1980s – Nathaniel Webb 978-1-78952-065-1
Van Morrison in the 1970s – Peter Childs – 978-1-78952-241-9
Mott the Hoople & Ian Hunter in the 1970s – John Van der Kiste 978-1-78-952-162-7
Pink Floyd In The 1970s – Georg Purvis 978-1-78952-072-9
Suzi Quatro in the 1970s – Darren Johnson 978-1-78952-236-5
Queen in the 1970s – James Griffiths 978-1-78952-265-5
Roxy Music in the 1970s – Dave Thompson 978-1-78952-180-1
Slade in the 1970s – Darren Johnson 978-1-78952-268-6
Status Quo in the 1980s – Greg Harper 978-1-78952-244-0
Tangerine Dream in the 1970s – Stephen Palmer 978-1-78952-161-0
The Sweet in the 1970s – Darren Johnson 978-1-78952-139-9
Uriah Heep in the 1970s – Steve Pilkington 978-1-78952-103-0
Van der Graaf Generator in the 1970s – Steve Pilkington 978-1-78952-245-7
Rick Wakeman in the 1970s – Geoffrey Feakes 978-1-78952-264-8
Yes in the 1980s – Stephen Lambe with David Watkinson 978-1-78952-125-2

Rock Classics Series
90125 by Yes – Stephen Lambe 978-1-78952-329-4
Bat Out Of Hell by Meatloaf – Geoffrey Feakes 978-1-78952-320-1
Bringing It All Back Home by Bob Dylan – Opher Goodwin 978-1-78952-314-0
Californication by Red Hot Chili Peppers - Matt Karpe 978-1-78952-348-5
Crime Of The Century by Supertramp – Steve Pilkington 978-1-78952-327-0

Also available from Sonicbond

The Dreaming by Kate Bush – Peter Kearns 978-1-78952-341-6
Let It Bleed by The Rolling Stones – John Van der Kiste 978-1-78952-309-6
Pawn Hearts by Van Der Graaf Generator – Paolo Carnelli 978-1-78952-357-7
Purple Rain by Prince – Matt Karpe 978-1-78952-322-5
The White Album by The Beatles – Opher Goodwin 978-1-78952-333-1

On Screen Series
Carry On... – Stephen Lambe 978-1-78952-004-0
David Cronenberg – Patrick Chapman 978-1-78952-071-2
Doctor Who: The David Tennant Years – Jamie Hailstone 978-1-78952-066-8
James Bond – Andrew Wild 978-1-78952-010-1
Monty Python – Steve Pilkington 978-1-78952-047-7
Seinfeld Seasons 1 to 5 – Stephen Lambe 978-1-78952-012-5

Other Books
1967: A Year In Psychedelic Rock 978-1-78952-155-9
1970: A Year In Rock – John Van der Kiste 978-1-78952-147-4
1972: The Year Progressive Rock Ruled The World – Kevan Furbank 978-1-78952-288-4
1973: The Golden Year of Progressive Rock 978-1-78952-165-8
Eric Clapton Sessions – Andrew Wild 978-1-78952-177-1
Dark Horse Records – Aaron Badgley 978-1-78952-287-7
Derek Taylor: For Your Radioactive Children – Andrew Darlington 978-1-78952-038-5
Ghosts – Journeys To Post-Pop – Matthew Restall 978-1-78952-334-8
The Golden Age of Easy Listening – Derek Taylor 978-1-78952-285-3
The Golden Road: The Recording History of The Grateful Dead – John Kilbride 978-1-78952-156-6
Hoggin' The Page – Groudhogs The Classic Years – Martyn Hanson 978-1-78952-343-0
Iggy and The Stooges On Stage 1967-1974 – Per Nilsen 978-1-78952-101-6
Jon Anderson and the Warriors – the Road to Yes – David Watkinson 978-1-78952-059-0
Magic: The David Paton Story – David Paton 978-1-78952-266-2
Misty: The Music of Johnny Mathis – Jakob Baekgaard 978-1-78952-247-1
Musical Guide To Red By King Crimson – Andrew Keeling 978-1-78952-321-8
Nu Metal: A Definitive Guide – Matt Karpe 978-1-78952-063-7
Philip Lynott – Renegade – Alan Byrne 978-1-78952-339-3
Remembering Live Aid – Andrew Wild 978-1-78952-328-7
Thank You For The Days - Fans Of The Kinks Share 60 Years of Stories – Ed. Chris Kocher 978-1-78952-342-3
The Sonicbond On Track Sampler – 978-1-78952-190-0
The Sonicbond Progressive Rock Sampler (Ebook only) – 978-1-78952-056-9
Tommy Bolin: In and Out of Deep Purple – Laura Shenton 978-1-78952-070-5
Maximum Darkness – Deke Leonard 978-1-78952-048-4
The Twang Dynasty – Deke Leonard 978-1-78952-049-1

Would you like to write for Sonicbond Publishing?

We are mainly a music publisher, but we also occasionally publish in other genres including film and television. At Sonicbond Publishing we are always on the look-out for authors, particularly for our two main series, On Track and Decades.

Mixing fact with in depth analysis, the On Track series examines the entire recorded work of a particular musical artist or group. All genres are considered from easy listening and jazz to 60s soul to 90s pop, via rock and metal.

The Decades series singles out a particular decade in an artist or group's history and focuses on that decade in more detail than may be allowed in the On Track series.

While professional writing experience would, of course, be an advantage, the most important qualification is to have real enthusiasm and knowledge of your subject. First-time authors are welcomed, but the ability to write well in English is essential.

Sonicbond Publishing has distribution throughout Europe and North America, and all our books are also published in E-book form. Authors will be paid a royalty based on sales of their book. Further details about our books are available from www.sonicbondpublishing.com. To contact us, complete the contact form there or email info@sonicbondpublishing.co.uk